Short-Cycle Assessment

Improving Student Achievement through Formative Assessment

Dr. Susan Lang
Todd Stanley
Betsy Moore

EYE ON EDUCATION
6 DEPOT WAY WEST, SUITE 106
LARCHMONT, NY 10538
(914) 833–0551
(914) 833–0761 fax
www.eyeoneducation.com

Library of Congress Cataloging-in-Publication Data

Lang, Susan. Short cycle assessment : improving student achievement through formative assessment / by Susan Lang, Todd Stanley, Betsy Moore.
    p. cm.
  ISBN 978-1-59667-073-0
1. Educational tests and measurements—United States. 2. Examinations—Design and construction. I. Stanley, Todd. II. Moore, Betsy. III. Title.
LB3051.L33 2008
371.26—dc22

                              2007043736

10 9 8 7 6 5 4 3 2

Also Available from EYE ON EDUCATION

Dedication

We would like to dedicate this book to the Ohio Center for Essential School Reform. Dr. Dan Hoffman founded the nonprofit organization 10 years ago. Dr. Hoffman began the Center with the principles of the Coalition of Essential Schools, a nationally recognized school reform movement with almost two decades of experience in providing leadership for school reform. Mr. Ed James joined the Ohio Center and developed the fundamentals of the short-cycle assessment process. Both educators were former administrators for the Reynoldsburg City School District in the Columbus, Ohio area. As Executive Director of the Center, Dr. Hoffman encouraged Dr. Lang's dissertation work and supported her efforts to make the study relevant for teachers and administrators.

Today, the Ohio Center for Essential School Reform serves school districts throughout the state of Ohio. The essential work focuses on formative assessment design. During the past 6 years the Center has further developed an Online Student Assessment System (OASIS), which tracks the formative assessment data ensuring easy analysis for teachers and administrators. We want to thank both founders for their vision and leadership for the Ohio Center for Essential School Reform.

The Authors

Meet the Authors

Dr. Susan Lang is the superintendent for the Rossford Exempted School District in the Toledo, Ohio area. She previously served as Executive Director of the Ohio Center for Essential School Reform where she and her staff worked with over 50 school districts to provide the conditions for academic success through the formative assessment process.

Dr. Lang had also served as the superintendent in Canal Winchester School District, secondary curriculum director in Mt. Healthy City Schools, technology director for Clermont County Educational Service center, principal for Medina City Schools, special education supervisor for Strongsville City Schools and teacher in the Bay Village Schools.

Dr. Lang has been selected on numerous occasions to speak nationally and state-wide on various topics such as Developing Business Partnerships, Leading with Data, Leadership through Differentiation and other current leadership topics. Her doctorate is from Miami University in Oxford, Ohio.

Dr. Lang has been recognized by her peers through the years as a bold, passionate, and sincere leader always striving to ensure each student's success. Canal Winchester named her the "Pillar of the Community," the Ohio superintendent's organization presented an Exemplary Leadership award to her on two separate occasions, and the Governor named her a Trailblazer in Ohio. She has three grown children, Suzanne, Michael, and Ashley.

Todd Stanley began teaching in 1997. Running the entire gamut, he taught 7th and 8th graders for five years, high school for three, elementary for two, and is currently teaching Social Studies and Science in a program for 5th and 6th grade gifted students for Reynoldsburg schools. He worked for the Christopher Program, an integrated project-based curriculum for juniors and seniors, and created the Ivy Program, a project-based gifted program for elementary students. He also spent three years working for the Ohio Center for Essential School Reform, training teachers in the state of Ohio how to create short-cycle assessments. He received his National Board Certification in 2000 and his gifted education certification in 2001. He lives in Pickerington, Ohio with his wife Nicki and two children, Anna and Abby.

Betsy Moore is a veteran teacher with over 30 years of experience who has been using short-cycle assessments since 1998. She began training teachers in the short-cycle assessment process in 2000 and has trained more than 1500 teachers in over 60 schools. Ms. Moore brings real experience and teacher-tried practices to the process, and has developed the process into one that is tailored to the needs of both teachers and students. Ms. Moore earned her Bachelor's Degree in Elementary and Special Education from Miami University and her Master's Degree in School Counseling from the University of Dayton. She is married and has two grown children. Ms. Moore lives with her husband, a high school administrator, in Columbus, Ohio.

Table of Contents

Introduction:
What is a Short-Cycle
Assessment?

Perhaps the most valuable result of all education is the ability to make yourself do the thing you have to do, when it ought to be done, whether you like it or not; it is the first lesson that ought to be learned; and however early a man's training begins, it is probably the last lesson that he learns thoroughly.

Thomas Huxley

The National Commission on Teaching and America's Future has expressed concern over the condition of America's teaching force. Linda Darling-Hammond (1999) argued the most significant predictor of success in student achievement in reading and mathematics is a well-qualified teacher. The question then becomes what is a well-qualified teacher? Traditional educational research often reveals itself not to have the effect on improving student achievement it once did. So what method does work? Teachers get their most important knowledge as situational decision makers. The formative assessment process came about from educators working on ways to accelerate student achievement and help predict how well students will perform on standards-based statewide tests. That leads us to the short-cycle assessment process and the benefits of using it.

What is a short-cycle assessment? It is a formative assessment given periodically, designed to help the teacher to shape or form instruction. This is not to be confused with a summative test. A summative test is a summation of what has been learned that is given at the end of a course or the end of the school year. It is the end of a process. Most state's summative assessments appear in the form of high-stakes tests that determine whether the student has mastered certain skills. Formative assessments on the other hand prepare students for the summative, showing strengths and weaknesses of skills that can be improved to ensure success.

The process of giving a short-cycle assessment involves working with professional learning communities to design a formative assessment process that examines student progress toward the mastery of content. A professional learning community can start with a single person. Like a stone thrown in a pond, if one teacher starts the process and garners results, the ripples could influence the rest of the professional community.

The primary aim of assessment is to determine whether a student has learned what they are supposed to learn. The short-cycle assessment process begins with the end in mind. Teachers examine what they want the students to be able to know and do, then shape instruction with this goal in mind. This short-cycle assessment process is rooted in the backwards building model of Grant Wiggins and Jay McTighe, emphasizing the concept of enduring understanding.

Throughout the educational process, assessment of students is a fundamental component of establishing the level of student achievement as well as evaluating the curriculum. Thus to promote effective learning, teachers must develop an approach that integrates short-term test preparation with long-term learning; something for which the short-cycle assessment process is designed. Just like students, teachers cannot be expected just to know these new methods at whim. According to Briscoe (1996), part of the change process for teachers is the creation of a personal curriculum for learning; that is, for changes to be implemented effectively, teachers must go through a retraining process that allows them to address the changes with confidence by integrating their own strengths as teachers.

The big question becomes what will this book do for you? *First it will teach you to write good questions that assess student learning.* Many times teachers are giving pedagogic techniques involving looking at the big picture, how to manage a classroom, or how to form essential questions. How much training is devoted to the writing of individual questions that assess what the student has learned? We as teachers write questions every day but do they do what we want them to do? Do the questions really assess that skill? Are they at the correct level of Bloom's taxonomy? Do they require the student to think the way we want students to think? By using the techniques in this book you will learn how to write questions that will do this. It will also teach you how to write quality assessments that lead to better instruction.

Second, this book will enable you to analyze and use data. Students have tons of information in their personal files that we busy educators never get the chance to get through, or if we do get through it, we do not know how to translate this to action in the classroom. The short-cycle assessment process provides simple, instant, usable data that can be used to shape your instruction so that no child truly gets left behind.

Most importantly this book will help you to improve student achievement. After all, the student is the entire reason we are here as educators. No matter how you feel about the high-stakes state testing, helping students pass a test that will determine whether they graduate or not is the means to an end. More importantly, it will make your students better thinkers and allow them to handle higher-level questioning skills that they will use well beyond their academic years.

The next logical question is how can this process be implemented in your own classroom? The process of short-cycle assessments is called the SCORE Process. We begin in Chapter 1 by looking at the rationale for why we should give short-cycle assessments and the framework behind it. What is the benefit for the teacher, students, administration, and district? Chapter 2 introduces the SCORE Process, the step-by-step process for understanding, writing, administering, and getting data from the short-cycle assessments. There are seven steps to the SCORE Process. Step 1 is an understanding by the teacher of the state standards addressed in Chapter 3. Sometimes these standards are called frameworks, courses of study, or core content, but the definition of a standard is a skill your state determines that every student who completes the course work for a particular grade level should master. Understanding these is extremely important because if the teacher does not know what they are, how on earth is the student going to be able to understand them?

Step 2 involves understanding the state assessments themselves. This means becoming familiar with the formatting of the state assessment and understanding how the different questions are formatted. Are they primarily multiple choice, are there constructed responses, and are there writing prompts for longer samples? Recognizing what the state uses and mimicking this in the classroom is very important to help with student success, and the focus of Chapter 4.

Once the standards are understood, the question becomes one of timing: When should each standard be taught? This is step 3 of the SCORE Process and involves the development of the pacing guide. A pacing guide maps out when to teach what and why. There are a couple of benefits to this, one being to ensure that all the standards are covered, and secondly, to plot out the standards so there is a logic to when you teach them. The pacing guide is covered in Chapter 5.

Step 4 is the actual development of the short-cycle assessment. This is the most involved of the steps, taking Chapters 6 and 7 to demonstrate. This involves learning how to write proper questions, how to format those questions, and how to assimilate them all together into an assessment. Almost as important as the writing of the assessment is the revising of it to ensure it is where it needs to be in order to determine student mastery.

The administration of the assessment is step 5, which is covered in Chapter 8. It is important to model the administration of the state test as much as possible. This includes length, testing environment, order of subjects, and other factors. The short-cycle assessment becomes the practice before the big game so you should try to prepare students for what they are going to see as much as possible.

Step 6 is also very involved and possibly the most important part of the process—data analysis. Now that these tests have been taken what do you do with the information gathered? Chapter 9 will show you how to look for gaps in the data, what questions to ask, and how to address these questions complete with possible solutions.

This leads to the central question to be addressed: How will your instruction change to focus on the information the assessment provided? This is step 7, instructional implications, and is discussed in Chapter 10. This ultimately will lead to improved student achievement.

One aspect to remember about the SCORE Process: This is not simply a theory that we wish to use you as a guinea pig to put into practice. This book is a collaboration between two classroom teachers and an administrator who are putting this theory into practice on a daily basis. It has been tried, modified, and used to great success with more than 50 school districts. This works, of that we are certain. If you are one of those people who need to see more proof, we have included a brief abstract of the study in Chapter 1. Dr. Susan Lang with Miami University of Oxford, Ohio completed her doctorate (*An Evaluation Study of Short-Cycle Assessments: An Instructional Process*) showing the improvements these districts made using the SCORE Process.

We have seen the results and experienced the growing pains that come with such an undertaking as short-cycle assessments. But one thing we will promise: If you follow the process, implement the strategies we suggest, and follow through with understanding the results; your students will reap the ultimate benefits.

Part I

An Introduction
to Short-Cycle Assessments

1

The Long and the Short of Short-Cycle Assessments

Teachers are expected to reach unattainable goals with inadequate tools. The miracle is that at times they accomplish this impossible task.

Haim G. Ginott

What is the Background Framework for this Work?

Professional development of teachers and improvement of their abilities have become frequent topics in the ongoing debate surrounding educational policy and reform. Schools, more than many professions, go through constant periods of change that require new training. The short-cycle assessment process came about from two approaches: the Objectives-Based Approach and Understanding by Design Model (UBD). Both approaches have a common ideology to the SCORE Process. With the focus on standards through a backward cycle, the SCORE Process promotes the essential questions in the collaborative learning community and data analysis sessions. This causes a teacher to contemplate *why* they teach instead of just *what* they teach.

Objectives-Based Approach

The objectives-based system does not by itself constitute an instructional program. Rather, it is intended to assist teachers in assessing students' skill development and in locating existing curricula that are appropriate to students' strengths and weaknesses. The idea upon which objectives-based systems are based is an appealing one. It asks the question of "wouldn't teachers' jobs be easier if they could find a simple way to monitor individual children's mastery of specific objectives and had access to appropriate instructional resources for teaching those objectives?" The success of the objectives-based system rests on several key variables though; the criterion-referenced tests must be reliable indicators of skill mastery, the testing, recording, and grouping requirements must be organized well enough so that teachers can implement them, and instructional materials or activities that are genuinely effective in teaching the specific comprehension skills must be identified.

1

Understanding by Design Model

Collaborative Learning (CL) is based on a process of teamwork in which students are encouraged to help each other gain a long-term understanding of important skills and concepts (Davidson, 1994). Understanding by Design (UBD) can then facilitate in improving academic outcomes within a CL setting. According to UBD pioneers Wiggins and McTighe (1998), the goal of the UBD approach is to help students retain knowledge more effectively by providing a memorable and personal learning experience. This is contrary to more traditional curriculum that tends to follow the progression of identifying objectives, implementing lesson plans, and then giving an assessment of results. Instead the UBD framework uses a "backward design process" that identifies assessments before planning learning experiences and lessons. This way the desired results can be more appropriately identified (Wiggins & McTighe, 1998).

The UBD model is centered on what are known as essential questions (EQs) for which simple "yes" or "no" or one word responses do not work. Instead, EQs are thought-provoking and necessitate complex answers. Within a CL setting, students can feed off of each other's responses to explore the topic on a deeper level (Wiggins & McTighe, 1998). This is one of the most efficient ways in which UBD and CL can work together to facilitate the experiential learning process.

According to Wiggins and McTighe, teachers should do whatever it takes to make it easier for students to focus on the "big picture," helping students understand what is really important. All too often teachers spend weeks on a particular unit and when assessment time arrives the teacher finds that many students did not grasp the "big picture." UBD asks teachers to determine what students should understand about a subject and then, working backward, develop lesson plans and assessment to help reach that goal. Wiggins and McTighe (1998) explain the benefits to this reversal as follows:

> Like other design professions, such as architecture, engineering, or graphic arts, designers in education must be mindful of their audiences. Professionals in these fields are strongly client centered. The effectiveness of their designs corresponds to whether they have accomplished their goals for the end users. Clearly, students are our primary clients, given that the effectiveness of curriculum, assessment, and instructional designs is ultimately determined by their achievement of desired learning (p.7).

There are overarching EQs that span an entire year and unit EQs. At the end of each unit students must demonstrate a competent answer to the EQs through a performance-based assessment. The power of this kind of design is it causes teachers to contemplate why they teach a particular lesson and keeps them from teaching it just because they "like it." This approach gives students the opportunity to act on their newly acquired knowledge and to show that they understand the true meaning (Davidson, 1994).

Within the Collaborative Learning context, the UBD approach helps to ensure that when students come together in groups, individual group members will make valuable contributions to the groups' understanding of key themes and ideas. By working backwards to determine desired outcomes, as well as by focusing on EQs, teachers can make the most efficient and effective use of collaboration and minimize wasted time and effort.

Finally, Professional Learning Communities offers a context for the process of SCORE. Richard Dufours' work establishes the profession of teaching as a continuation of learning within the context of improvement. Critical friends group (CFG) within school buildings has been an effective way of studying successful best practices. The SCORE Process encourages the collaboration and professional learning time with teachers to develop assessments that are common and review data to change instructional practices.

As SCORE is implemented in a building(s) and/or district, changes occur within a teacher's skill set as well as their attitudes the further along they are in the process. Many times when innovation and change begins there is a negative perception until success and understanding is acquired by the majority of the staff. The models/approaches mentioned above set a framework for the short-cycle assessment process and offer an understanding to the "big idea" behind the strategy for achievement.

What are Short-Cycle Assessments?

Short-cycle assessments are tests given several times over the course of the school year with the intention of preparing students for the high-stakes test. Almost all states give a test designed to assess students on what they have learned based on the content standards that state has deemed necessary. These tests can take many different formats including written responses, multiple-choice, or a demonstration of learning.

So why the need for short-cycle assessments? Imagine taking a course in college where all the homework you did, all the presentations you gave, and all the class discussion you participated in meant nothing. The only thing that will determine your grade for that course is going to be the pencil-to-paper test given over the course of 1 week. This is daunting enough when you have a 10-week class. Now imagine a 35-week-long course. How intimidating is that?

That is what public schools are doing. All the work a student does in class does not mean anything compared to the state assessment. The student may have demonstrated mastery of a particular skill time and time again over the course of a class but if the student bubbles or fills in the wrong answer circle on the high-stakes test, as far as the state is concerned, the student is deficient in that skill.

As an administrator why would you want to wait to see how your students did on the state test? Wouldn't it make more sense for the teacher of that class to offer tests every few weeks using the same format so that students are completely prepared for the final? This would act as a good predictor of how students are going to perform. The short-cycle assessment process is like going to a baseball game. While you are engaged in the game you watch how the innings play out. You don't just wait for the ending score; instead, you keep track of the score inning by inning. That's what short-cycle assessments are. They are written in the same format and cover the same content as the final assessment, only in smaller pieces. Suddenly that final assessment does not seem so daunting but simply the final puzzle that you've been putting pieces into all year long. Hence short-cycle assessments are a tool to prepare students for the final assessment. Some people claim this to be "teaching to the test" as though this were an educational equivalent to a curse word. If you are one of those people who feel this way, read the argument in *Teaching to the Test* (p. 121). It might convince you otherwise.

Enduring Understanding

The purpose of the state test is to determine whether the student truly understands the concept of the skills required for that grade level. Students have become very adept at playing the game of school. How many times have you memorized the information you needed for a test long enough to sit down, spew it out, and then forget it forever? This creates an issue when that same student is expected to answer a question based on that information many months later and is unable to do so. If a student does poorly on the high-stakes test, does this mean you are a bad teacher or that you wasted your time teaching a subject? The real question you need to ask yourself is did students get an enduring understanding with the teaching method you used or were they able to play the game of school where grades become much more important than learning?

The state achievement tests require that students understand something not just that year, but also several years later. A student might have to dig deep and remember a concept from the 7th grade just to answer a question on the 10th grade assessment. The question to consider is how confident are you that students understand what you teach in class to the point that they would be able to relate this understanding several years later? This is especially important when you have a group that sometimes cannot remember math concepts from one school year to the next because of the summer layoff or who struggle to tell you the difference between homophones and homographs because they sound the same.

There will be potential roadblocks along the way. For instance, have you ever had a teacher in a grade level higher than yours come up to you to let you know that you need to teach the students "this and that" so that they can be more successful in their class? Most times your knee-jerk reaction is, "But I taught that, and taught that, and taught that?" What happened? Why can't the students do it? One very real possibility is that there is a distinct difference between teaching and learning. We can teach everything and "cover" it in a given year, but if the students do not learn it, what is the point? One of the biggest mistakes we make as educators is that often we keep doing the same thing even if it isn't getting us the results we want. If there is something that you know you have "taught," but the students have not "learned," consider doing something different—teach it in a different way, use a different method, etc. After all, Albert Einstein said it best when he said, "We cannot solve problems with the same thinking we used when we created the problems." In other words, "We can't expect different results if we don't do something different."

With these high-stakes tests the state is now saying not only do we have to teach this stuff, but the students actually have to learn it. That may sound facetious but we all know as educators that students have a funny way of determining what they will and will not understand. It comes down to the old adage of "you can lead a horse to water but you can't make it drink." How long do we have to hold our students' heads underwater until they decide to take that drink? How do we get them to understand?

The SCORE Process uses a goal-setting theory embedded in the change process by directing teachers to work with the end in mind. They constantly obtain feedback so they can determine whether they are succeeding in teaching the standards successfully to their students (Locke & Latham, 1990). It is assumed that the teacher will develop a deeper understanding of standards-based assessment, use data from the standards-based assessment to monitor student performance on the short assessments, and make instructional implications in the classroom based on the data from the assessments. The assess–plan–teach process is cyclical and always evolving as teachers become more comfortable with using assessments in their instructional practice.

The Benefits of Short-Cycle Assessments

Although we will go over most of this in far greater detail as the book goes on, here are some benefits of short-cycle assessments:

- Short-cycle assessments will help you find out exactly where each of your students fall with regards to the Content Standards in your state, and therefore better prepare them for the high-stakes test.
- Short-cycle assessments will give you information ahead of time, instead of waiting until the results of the high-stakes tests come out.
- Short-cycle assessments can show a year's growth by comparing last year's assessment scores with this year's assessment scores.
- Short-cycle assessments require an enduring understanding of the material that has been taught.
- Short-cycle assessments show teaching strengths and areas for improvement.
- Short-cycle assessments are what is best for kids—bottom line.

The last one, what is best for kids, can sometimes be a sore spot for some teachers. How can testing these kids so much be what is best for them? The simple answer to that is for a student to graduate, in many states the student must pass a graduation exam. Sure one of our main goals as teachers is to see to it students learn, but isn't the ancillary purpose from the kindergarten teacher all the way through junior high and senior year to make sure these students receive a high school diploma? Short-cycle assessments are a tool to ensure this happens more often than not.

The Four Es

Broken down even further, short-cycle assessments give some clear advantages that we like to call the Four Es:

1. To give planned and purposeful *exposure* to the benchmarks, indicators, and formats.
2. To build resilience and *endurance* for each student to be able to (a) sit through the test and (b) work through difficult questions.
3. To develop *expertise* in each teacher's ability to ask higher-level questions, base instructional decisions for delivery on performance data, and collaborate for curricular direction across grade levels.
4. To *empower* students and their parents to become responsible decision makers for learning.

Taking these and breaking them down even further, *exposure* can be a very powerful tool. Statistics show a majority of students do better on the SAT or ACT exams when they take it a second time. Why is this? Have students become smarter between tests? Have they developed new areas of their brains unbeknownst to them previously? Is it because they have been willing to pay for the test two times and the testing company slips them an easier test? The real reason is because students have been *exposed* to the test once already and are familiar with the format and types of questions it asks. Before they might have been tripped up on the wording of the question or the format in which they have to answer it, not the actual content or skill being asked. The second time through it becomes more about the content and less about the format. Looking at exposure through a sports context, this is why coaches have their athletes participate in scrimmages or practice games. That way, they will be familiar with the athletic contest before the real one occurs. It is also why English teachers cringe when a student turns in their rough draft as their final paper. It is obvious they did not take a second look at the paper and it shows. Short-cycle assessments can be viewed as rough drafts preparing for the final draft, which is the state assessment.

To test this theory, try the *Testing Twice* (p. 123) activity. In this you will be taking a test twice, once when you are unfamiliar with the formatting, and the second time after you become more comfortable with the formatting. The idea is to see which test you feel more comfortable taking, and thus work more quickly and with greater consistency. Ask yourself if the two are related. How does this correlate to your own students?

Short-cycle assessments are written in the same format as the state test with similar vocabulary that exposes students to the point where they are no longer tripped up if a question has two parts or four. They have learned to recognize this and are merely being evaluated on their knowledge.

Endurance is important because it is difficult enough to get students to sit still over the course of a 30-minute class period much less for several hours over the course of a few days. Once again students are penalized for something other than their understanding of the skill. If a student begins to bottom out of their patience an hour into the assessment, all questions answered after this first hour will be affected. That is not a true measure of what a student knows.

Consider when (what time of the day, what day of the week, etc.) the assessment is given. If your assessment is given on the last day of a busy week, one of two things might happen: (a) because students have become used to the testing and its formatting, they will do better, or (b) students have become so burned out by so much testing that their brains are fried and cannot possibly give it their all. Which scenario occurs depends, of course, on the student.

Short-cycle assessments build the endurance and tolerance of students. Because they have become used to sitting still over an extended period of time to take the short-cycle assessments it is not so much of a stretch to sit for a couple of hours and take the state test. If you model your schedule to give the short-cycle assessments for each subject area over the course of a week, students will be even more tolerant of having to do the same at test time.

Expertise comes in the form of the teacher's ability to relate lessons to the content standards and in asking higher-level, state-assessment-like questions. Short-cycle assessments will require the teacher to become very familiar with the state Content Standards, and the way those standards are instructed and assessed. Through writing short-cycle assessments and going over the questions in class, the teacher's expertise on how to instruct and assess will improve.

Imagine you are a teacher introducing a new lesson you have never taught before and like lots of teachers you have to teach the same class five times in a day. Your morning class is the guinea pig because you are teaching the lesson for the first time. You are bound to fumble here and there, making mistakes galore, and trying out different techniques, some which lead to dead-ends. By the time you get to the next class it is more of a dress rehearsal where you have practiced it at least once, still making some mistakes but not nearly as many, and the performance is a little more refined. The afternoon classes get the best possible education you have to offer because you have done the lesson a couple of times, all the kinks have been worked out, and you have even added some things you have learned from the other two classes.

The reason for this is because you had enough familiarity with the lesson to be at your best. You can adjust the flow to the level of the class because you are comfortable enough to do that and can push the students to a higher level of thinking because you know the lesson well enough. Your expertise is at a point that you can be at your best.

The simple fact is that teachers often have to teach skills they are not comfortable with or do not fully understand. We can't all be as all-powerful and all-knowing as students or the state expect us to be, especially elementary teachers who have to know all subject areas in a far greater range than the more secularized high school classes. Even though we often have to teach things that are not our strengths, the more familiar we become with them, the more this becomes a strength because familiarity often breeds understanding.

The same goes with a familiarity of the Content Standards in your state. As we gain deeper understanding, the easier it is to work them into the day-to-day activities of the classroom seamlessly as well as the vocabulary of the test itself. Higher level questioning is not something most people can just do cold; they have to be comfortable enough with the content in order to take it to the next level. That is what teachers creating the short-cycle assessments get from the process—a comfort with the standards.

The last and most important advantage to the short-cycle process is the *empowerment* that comes when students realize they are as responsible for their educational success as their teachers. As students begin to rack up small success after small success from the short-cycle assessments they gain the confidence to tackle the much larger high-stakes test.

Many of the schools who use short-cycle assessments experience this same scenario; the first time students take a written portion of the test, students either leave the response blank, draw a picture, or even simply write "I don't know." More often than not, the reason for this is that the students don't feel empowered to answer the question. Because they don't understand, their first reaction is to shut down. Leaving the answer blank is much easier than trying to answer and failing—at least in their mind. When the second assessment comes around, students are writing a word or two, sometimes maybe even a fragmented sentence. It still is very poor but it is better than before. By the time the fourth assessment is given students have become empowered in the process enough to attempt writing a legitimate answer. They feel confident enough to try even if they are not successful. They have become empowered enough in their learning to take a chance.

Because teachers have communicated the results of the short-cycle assessments to parents and what their particular student needs to do to improve, parents also are given a sense of empowerment to help where they see fit. It is no longer just up to the teacher to see that the student passes—the parent also may take a larger role.

The Short of Why

Short-cycle assessments give students the practice and teachers the position to ensure success on the state assessment, which in most cases signifies learning. Just like a football coach trying to defeat another team, the coach familiarizes himself with the opponents, looks at film of past games, reads scouting reports, and teaches his players how to handle adversity. Success is not coincidental. It is through this practice that victory comes on game night, not just hoping the night of the game everyone can pull it all together. It becomes a very intentional act.

The Short Version of the Proof

The study completed with Miami University, Oxford, Ohio and Dr. Susan Lang titled, *An Evaluation Study of Short-Cycle Assessments: An Instructional Process* evaluated the Literacy Curriculum Alignment Process (LCAP), presently titled SCORE. The study was the foundation of this book. Dr. Lang's evaluation study determined if the school districts that adopted the process showed improvement on measures for the Ohio Academic Content Standards after 2 years. LCAP is defined as an intensive literacy-based professional development program. The process was developed to introduce principals and their leadership teams to an array of instructional tools, including the backwards-building curriculum from standards, curriculum alignment, mapping, assessment practices, and data analysis protocols. The primary focus of the process is to work with professional learning communities to design a formative assessment program that monitors student progress towards the mastery of literacy and numeracy standards.

This study examined the SCORE Process using an objectives-based evaluation model. A series of questions were proposed and the achievement was gathered through both qualitative (proximate) and quantitative (distal) methods. The quantitative findings indicate an improvement on the Ohio standardized tests in fourth and sixth grades in 53 buildings of 20 Ohio public school districts. The qualitative data were generated through a series of questions posed to respondents in a survey through focus groups. Emergent themes were prevalent in the analysis of surveys, feedback forms, and focus groups. Themes included how teachers learn of standards and state tests; teacher perception for the rationale for the short-cycle assessments and critical thinking; teachers' and students' preparation and anxiety level for the tests; instruction/curriculum changes because of test performance; teachers' accounts of needing reflection and collaboration time; teacher perception of new educational initiatives with a short-term fix; and teacher utilization of data analysis. Several positive changes in perception regarding the teachers' views of standard-based assessment were found.

Theoretical Base

Educational research must develop case knowledge that examines teachers' actions and decisions in different contexts and with diverse kinds of learners (Cochran-Smith & Lytle, 1993). Reformers can construct knowledge with teachers who help develop these cases of practice and interpret data from detailed data of their students' performance. Research that engages teachers improves the responsiveness of research to realities of teaching while developing the kind of thinking teachers must use to evaluate information continually about students, practice, and instructional effects. *This research study offers information related to teacher responsiveness to short-cycle assessment data to help drive improved instructional practices affecting student achievement.*

Professional development and teacher involvement in assessment design are important components. *The primary goal is to change what and how teachers teach rather than to measure performance for accountability purposes.* A program's theory of change identifies "program resources, program activities and intended program outcomes and specifies a chain of causal assumptions linking program resources, activities, and intermediate outcomes, and ultimate goals" (Wholey, 1987, p. 78).

Methodological Approach

The evaluation study involved collecting 20 districts' achievement scores from 1999 to 2004 and comparing the scores of the same grade level of students. This provided information on the impact of the program but did not look at individual student performance. Data were analyzed regarding the impact of the SCORE

Process on student achievement. Figures 1.1 and 1.2 represent the average test gains made in the districts in the 4th and 6th grades and the year following the completion of the study the additional gains.

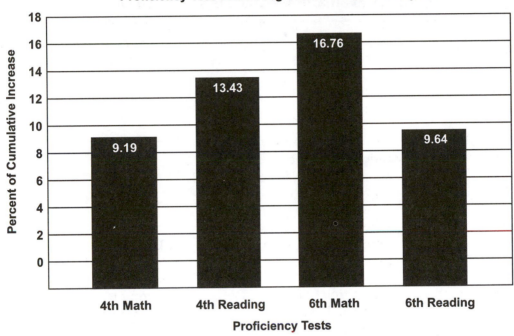

Figure 1.1 Average Overall Gains

Proficiency Test Score Progress Since LCAP Inception

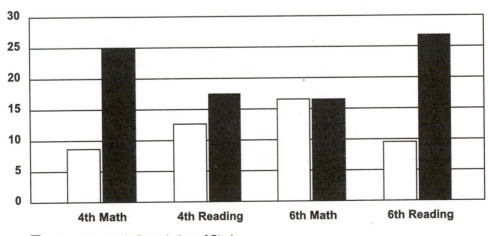

Figure 1.2 Comparison Study Gains

☐ Gains Through Completion of Study
■ 05-06 Additional Gains

Did the SCORE Process change teacher perceptions and practices regarding standards-based assessment? The chart below represents the specific questions asked so as to gain an understanding of teachers' perceptions. Surveys, feedback forms and focus groups were completed and analyzed. Figure 1.3 identifies the key themes that came from the data.

Figure 1.3 Evaluation Model Summary on Outcomes

Data Sources	Emerging Themes	Impact on Decision Making for Future SCORE Work
"Where Are We?" Surveys	1. How teachers learn of standards and state tests.	Early exposure to the process is desired.
Feedback Forms	2. Teacher perception for the rationale for the short cycle assessments and critical thinking.	Same as #1
Focus Groups	3. Teachers' and students' preparation and anxiety level for the tests.	Practice builds confidence and endurance.
All 3 sources	4. Instruction/curriculum changes due to test performance.	Engaging teachers in the process and providing collaboration time to make instructional changes.
All 3 sources	5. Teachers' accounts of needing reflection and collaboration time.	Building administrators need to provide time for data analysis.
All 3 sources	6. Teacher perception of new educational initiatives with a short-term fix.	Fewer initiatives in the building, and time to learn and practice new strategies.
All 3 sources	7. Teacher utilization of data analysis.	Practice in the process and leadership in providing the guidance and resources for use of data.

2

The SCORE Process

Quality is never an accident; it is always the result of high intention, sincere effort, intelligent direction, and skillful execution; it represents the wise choice of many alternatives.

Willa A. Foster

The SCORE Process is a system we developed to implement the short-cycle assessment process. When it was initially rolled out, it was called LCAP or Literacy Curriculum Alignment Project and its main focus was improving student literacy. Although the SCORE Process can be started with a single teacher, the way we used the SCORE assess–plan–teach cycle was in a three-phase process. The first phase was an orientation to prepare a school for change. This phase began with developing teacher knowledge of the Content Standards as well as the state assessments. This was accomplished in several activities with the full staff. Activities included going over curriculum maps, student performance statements of evidence of Content Standards, and discussion among teachers and administrators about what evidence would be seen if a student were demonstrating understanding of particular Content Standards.

The second phase was implementation. The process directed teachers to discuss what evidence is needed to determine a student's mastery on each Content Standard. This discussion led to the development of a pacing guide. The pacing guide was used to distribute the standards into short-cycled time frames for the four 9-week instructional periods. Following the development of the pacing guide, the teachers began to design assessments aligned to the Content Standards for each of the periods on their pacing guide. This step involved the composition of the assessments, such as the type of questions and level of questions. Considerable time was invested in working with teachers with Bloom's taxonomy and how to ask and write high-level and critical thinking type questions. Using the writing process, assessments were developed by teachers for each of the grading periods. Particular attention was given to writing questions of moderate to high complexity.

Teacher written assessments of the Content Standards then served to drive the instruction for that period, thus initiating the assess–plan–teach cycle. Following the administration of the short-cycle assessment, the teachers were led through a process of data analysis. The teachers learned to analyze individual, classroom, and district performance, and how these results related to needed changes in classroom practice.

Armed with reports on each student and each class, teachers were able to plan instruction with new understandings of both individual and class performance.

The third phase of SCORE was to build capacity. Through a mix of grade-level meetings, teachers refined lesson planning, conducted data meetings with predictive information on student assessment during the year, and differentiated student work based on data. Principals were able to look at building-wide trends and identify sources of strength and areas in need of growth. Superintendents also looked at data by studying the same scan from building to building.

Throughout the process, teachers collaborated and shared intervention strategies, successful best practices, and lesson ideas. Using the data some school districts chose to revise their curricula maps. The assess–plan–teach process is cyclical and continues in a fluid manner, always evolving as teachers become more and more comfortable with their own assessment and data driven instructional decisions.

We soon discovered, however, that this process could be applied to any content area from Math and Science to Social Studies, as well as the related arts. As a result of this, the process was renamed SCORE which stands for

S   *Short*

C   *Cycle Assessments*

O   *Organized for*

R   *Results and*

E   *Expectations*

The short cycle of the process was defined in the Introduction and Chapter 1. Consequently, we will start with the third part of the SCORE Process.

Organized

The idea of short-cycle assessments is not enough. There needs to be a clear, *organized* plan for the administration of the assessments as well as the analysis of the results, otherwise they will not be effective in helping students to prepare for the state assessment.

The reason this process needs to be organized is simple; imagine you are teaching a dance class. Your final assessment is a recital where students will show off everything they learned during the course of the class. You simply cannot come into the class and tell students to create their own dances and then at the end, put it all together into a routine. You would have some people dancing ballet, other people jazz, and others hip-hop, all to a different rhythm and beats with no one in sync—in other words you would have a giant mess at the end. Similarly, in your academic classroom, even though students are invariably at different levels, you have to set goals of learning that each student either meets or exceeds and teach them the skills to get them to that point. You cannot just teach them whatever you like and hope they are able to put it all together come the high-stakes test. Once the class reaches the point of mastery, short-cycle assessments are given to determine whether or not individual students have mastered that skill. If they have, celebrate your success. If they have not, you need to develop a strategy to ensure students have truly mastered what it is you have taught them.

The frequent reaction from teachers at this point is, "Wait a minute. I know my students mastered this skill. I gave my own assessment (maybe even both written and performance) and they did just fine. Just because they don't perform well on an assessment aligned to the high-stakes test doesn't mean they don't know the information."

The problem with this way of thinking is, like it or not, many times both students and teachers are judged by the way the students perform on the high-stakes test. If you look at short-cycle assessments as a piece of the puzzle, or just a different way to show mastery, that may help you with preparing them to be successful on the state test. It isn't about one way being right and one way being wrong; it's about what is best for the students. Ultimately, being able to show mastery on the state test is good for our students—the same way that being able to apply that skill, perform that skill, understand that skill, and maybe even teach that skill is.

The method that best organizes this process is Stiggins' backwards building approach. The idea here is you begin with the end in mind, and work your way backwards. In that dance class, you create the final recital routine first, determine what skills need to be taught in order for the students to do it, figure out when to teach those skills, and along the way assess whether the students have mastered that skill to ensure they can perform at the end. In the SCORE Process, you take the final state assessment as your beginning, break down what skills students have to know in order to be successful on the test, determine how and when to teach those skills, figure out how you will assess along the way, and plot this out over the course of the school year.

Broken down, backwards building looks like this:

Backwards Building Process

1. *Identify* what you want to *accomplish.*
2. *Determine* the *product* that will show what you learned.
3. *Plan* how you will *develop* this product.

The problem becomes, how do we know what the state test is going to look like when it hasn't been given yet? Most states have been kind enough to offer Content Standards that the test will be based on. Even though we cannot know exactly what is going to be on the test, we do know what standards most likely will be represented. By understanding those standards we have given our students the best chance possible to be successful on the state assessment.

Results

Results are extremely important to the process and yet they become the most neglected in a lot of cases. As teachers we are given lots of data, enough to choke a horse and probably several members of the horse's immediate family. If you go to any student file you will find tons of data. The question becomes twofold: (a) As a teacher do you understand what this data is and how to use it? and (b) Do you have the time to go through every student file to glean what information you need? One of the best aspects of the SCORE Process is that the information you get is simple, immediate, and most important, usable.

The analysis of this data is covered in much more detail in Chapter 9, but here is a brief overview of the things it will allow you to do:

- You will see where students are

- Where they need to go

- How to group your students by readiness level not just in one general subject like math or English, but by specific skills

- Who suffers from test anxiety

- Who has ability but does not put forth the effort

- What type or format of question your students struggle with the most

Using the results to figure out things like this will enable you as the teacher to adjust your teaching accordingly and ensure the students are "getting it."

Expectations

The million-dollar question then becomes, what do you do with these results? This should manifest itself in the *expectations* the teacher has of his or her students. If students have shown mastery in a certain Content Standard, a teacher should expect students to maintain that mastery throughout the school year, reinforcing it with activities and lessons. Teachers should expect all students to be able to write constructed responses, even if they have shown the contrary in their previous testing experiences. We should expect 100% from 100% of the students. That doesn't mean we are going to get it, but expecting it is something very different.

The results of the short-cycle assessments allow you to set the bar for these expectations. If you see your students are struggling with a certain skill, the expectation should be that you will see improvement in this skill and put into place the practices that will allow this improvement to occur.

Isn't it ironic that every year, new world records are broken? Even though people have been setting these records for decades, someone always comes along and is able to best it even though it would seem to be the highest achievement a person could ever accomplish. Why are we able to consistently best the past record? Isn't there somewhere we will eventually plateau and no longer be able to overcome? The answer in most cases seems to be "no" because we see a goal and expect to set out and achieve or even exceed that goal. That is what has to happen in the classroom.

The SCORE Cycle

For those people who are visual and like to look at the big picture, Figure 2.1 is the SCORE Process diagrammed. As you can see, it begins with an understanding of the state Content Standards and the state assessment itself (see Chapters 3 and 4). Once you have those, you jump right into the circle, designing what we call a pacing guide (Chapter 5), creating the assessment (Chapters 6 and 7), giving it (Chapter 8), analyzing the results (Chapter 9), making modifications in the classroom (Chapter 10), and repeating the process all over again.

Figure 2.1 The SCORE Process

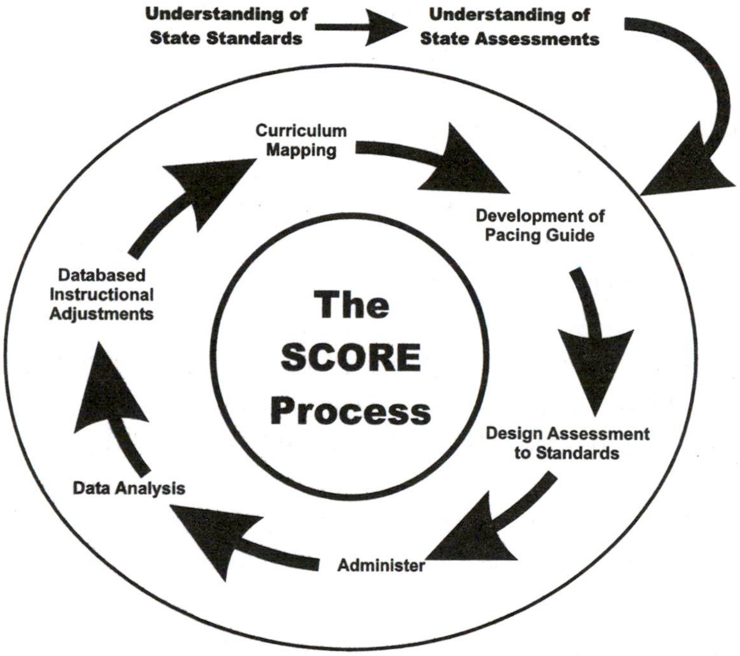

The SCORE cycle itself always remains the same, but the implementation of the process and procedures can be adapted to fit the needs of your school. How many times you decide to give the test, in what capacity, in what subject areas, all of these are dependent on the needs of the school and what sort of improvement you want to see. This Chapter gives the typical implementation strategy, but also discusses alternatives to be considered. To figure out what strategy would be best for your particular school, complete the worksheet *Figuring Out Which SCORE Model Works Best for You* (p. 126).

When to Test

The typical implementation for the SCORE Process is to give the short-cycle assessments four times, at the end of each 9 weeks quarter. It would look something like Figure 2.2.

Figure 2.2 SCORE Process Timeline

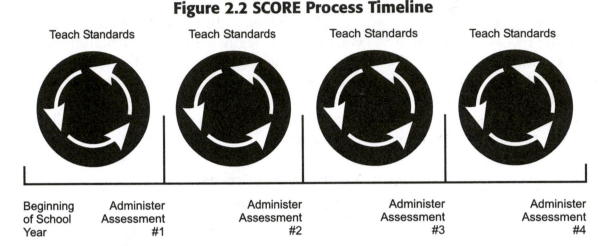

| Teach Standards | Teach Standards | Teach Standards | Teach Standards |

| Beginning of School Year | Administer Assessment #1 | Administer Assessment #2 | Administer Assessment #3 | Administer Assessment #4 |

Some schools have grading periods divided into 6-week increments so you could conceivably give six short-cycle assessments; others have trimesters that would require only three assessments. The question is whether you want to break the assessments into the different grading periods or not, as well as how often you want the information that short-cycle assessments can provide.

Something to consider is if you give too many assessments you cost instructional time and may even incur burnout in the students and the teachers as well. Four assessments a year allows enough of a gap for students to learn new skills and standards as well as addressing the other concern some teachers have of testing students too much.

It is usually at this point we hear teachers say, "I am testing my kids so much, I don't have time to teach." There are three things to consider with regard to this statement.

1. You already constantly assess your students through observation, performance assessments, informal assessments, quizzes, assignments, etc. Assessment is actually already as much a part of your day as is instruction.

2. If you do not assess your students, how do you know they have learned what it is you taught them? You can teach a dog to sit up, but if he cannot do it, you have wasted a lot of time teaching him. Assessment ensures learning has taken place.

3. We as teachers often are not as good as giving up unnecessary practices as we should be. If we have something we really enjoy teaching but the state

does not consider a standard, we stick with it anyway because we are comfortable with it. If you implement short-cycle assessments, they may be able to take the place of some of your current assessments. Don't be afraid to throw out some of the old to make room for the new. We use the statement "weed the garden" when discussing this practice.

Another approach we have implemented in some schools is the idea of pre- and posttests. You decide what standards are going to be tested over the course of the time period, give a pretest to see how much students already know about the standards and adjust your instruction accordingly, focusing heavily on the standards students did not show mastery of and reinforcing those they did. Then give a posttest with different questions designed to determine whether they have now gained mastery or enduring understanding of the standards.

Whichever approach you choose you should try to be consistent throughout the district. The rationale for this is that if you are conducting short-cycle assessments in each grade level, the pieces of the puzzle have to be able to fit together smoothly. That would be hard to do that if the pieces do not match.

What to Test

The next logical question is in what subject areas and grade levels should testing occur? SCORE can be rolled out in several different ways. If you are a classroom teacher trying to implement this with your own students, find the method that works best for your style of teaching. If you are a school trying to figure out across the district in what subject areas and grade levels to use this process, there are several options.

When it comes to grade levels we typically will implement the SCORE Process K–10. The rationale for this is that in many states, students begin taking the state assessment by the 3rd grade. By beginning in kindergarten, students will have been doing this for a few years and will be better prepared when they take the state assessment for the first time, sort of like hitting the ground running. The 10th grade is usually the target grade for the graduation test, as most states give students multiple opportunities to pass. Therefore, we propose limiting the short-cycle assessment process to grade 10, at least for most students. Using the SCORE Process with any students who do not pass the state test on the first try, or even with all students to show mastery of learning, is certainly an option that we would advocate.

Some schools choose to only focus on their elementary levels while others want to focus on just the high school because that is where they are the most deficient. What you must decide is what the best fit for your school is. A big advantage of implementing the process across all grade levels is that students continue to get practice with the formatting and questioning techniques even if there is not an achievement test for that grade level. If you were to skip certain grade levels, students might get out of practice and struggle when they have to take state assessments again. Math teachers, as well as those who teach foreign languages, know if students take any extended period time off of these areas, it is typically hard to just simply jump back into it. There needs to be continual reinforcement of the skills to keep students sharp. This applies to assessments as well as instruction.

Another advantage is that teachers can pass the strengths and weaknesses of their students taken from the short-cycle assessments to the next grade-level teacher who, in turn, can use the information gained to create the best learning experience for the students. This encourages collaboration between grade levels and can lead to vertical alignment where teachers smoothly hand off a student to the level above them without the gaps of information that can sometimes happen from year to year in a school.

As far as what subject areas to assess, that too depends on the fit for the school. When we go into a school we generally recommend the core subject areas of English, Math, Science, and Social Studies because it matches up with the assessments the state gives in most cases. Some schools will choose only to focus on a particular subject area they are having difficulty with such as math or reading. We have other districts that have the short-cycle assessments in every single class, including related arts programs like music, art, and physical education. The rationale is that students become familiar with the formatting and higher level questions in every subject area, not just the core ones. It also brings legitimacy to the related arts courses where many teachers feel slighted because schools focus so much on the core areas due to the high-stakes testing. This lets the students know that *all* courses are important and the expectations will be set high across the board.

In the course of the years implementing the SCORE Process we have seen assessments for all foreign language classes, including German and Latin, technology courses such as keyboarding, marketing, and industrial design, art courses at all grade levels, music electives such as basic guitar and marching band, and even woodshop, home economics, and business classes. The lesson we learned from this is that short-cycle assessments can apply to any course, even ones that tend to be more performance based. The way to create assessments for such courses is to set up scenarios where the students would normally apply a hands-on approach and then ask questions about the approach they would use. Obviously for an art class where the student produces artistic works, it would be difficult to have the students show the same creativity in a multiple-choice question, but the techniques used to produce such a piece and the thought process can be captured in a short-cycle assessment to give you a snapshot of their abilities. This is also a way to allow the students to compare components of the subject—such as art students comparing art pieces or even artists. The same way that we argue that students need to be assessed in different ways, we could argue that only assessing in a performance style could be just as limiting as only assessing in a formal paper and pencil test.

How to Test

You should try to model whatever method your state uses for its assessment as much as possible. If students must take the state assessment over the course of a week, a test a day, model that in your short-cycle-assessment schedule. Similarly, if the state gives two tests a day, one per half day, shadow that approach. The idea is that familiarity breeds understanding so making the process as familiar as possible for the students will be beneficial.

Where we have seen the process break down is when districts tell their teachers to give the short-cycle assessments whenever they find it convenient without a set schedule for the building or district. What tends to happen is that some teachers never get around to giving it or give it so late that there are only a couple of weeks left before the next one, defeating the purpose of taking the results from the assessment to set expectations for the next grading period. This also skews the validity of the assessment. That is why we have found that consistency across the building or district is the more effective way to go.

The Short of the SCORE Process

The SCORE Process allows for meaningful diagnostic testing to take place with immediate and useable data derived from teacher generated tests. Every school finds the implementation that best fits their needs whether it is in certain subject areas, certain grade levels, or across the entire school. Whatever the approach, the process for executing SCORE is the same; being organized and getting the results you want and using them to see the expectations you need for your students to achieve at the highest possible level.

3

Understanding the Content Standards

The foundation of every state is the education of its youth.

Diogenes Laertius

Clarifying What a Standard Is

Almost every state has content and skills required of every student in a particular grade level and subject area. Each state has its own names for these content and skills. Here are most of them:

- Courses of Study
- Academic Standards
- Curriculum Frameworks
- Model Content Standards
- Quality Core Curriculum Standards
- Achievement Standards
- Performance Descriptors
- Learning Standards
- Curricular Standards
- Core Content
- Learning Results
- Education Content
- Benchmarks
- Standard Course of Study
- Priority Academic Student Skills
- Essential Knowledge and Skills

- Essential Academic Learning Requirements
- Instructional Goals and Objectives
- Curriculum Guides
- Sunshine State Standards
- Standards of Learning

Because there are so many terms for this set of required content and skills, in this book we simplify them all into the term *Content Standards*. Depending on the state in which you reside, mentally insert the term that applies whenever we use our general term of Content Standards. By standardizing these terms we hope to make this book both easier to follow and more useful for teachers across the United States.

Why Standards?

The rationale for having Content Standards is to insure consistency among teachers. You wouldn't want a 5th grade Social Studies teacher who loves to teach about Egypt spending the entire year covering this, only to have the 6th grade teacher who also is fascinated with Egypt, cover it again. Meanwhile the student has learned nothing about American history, which is necessary for success in the 7th grade. The standards are designed to vertically align so that teachers getting a student can be confident that the student has gotten the necessary lessons that act as a prerequisite for their class. So a math teacher can teach a more advanced lesson because the student learned the basics for it the year before.

We often hear from teachers that the Content Standards is the state dictating to them how to teach. We make it clear to these teachers that the Content Standards indicate only *what* you are teaching. They say nothing about *how* you go about doing this. Let us say that again because that is a very important distinction. *The Content Standards do not tell you how to teach; they only indicate what you need to cover.* How you teach this content is completely up to you, the individual teacher. This means teachers can design lessons covering the Content Standards that benefit their strengths as a teacher. For instance, if lecture is the style that is most effective for you, you can design the Content Standards to fit into a lecture format. If hands-on activities are more your style, then create lesson plans that allow students to learn the Content Standards using such activities. The Content Standards will only stifle your creativity as a teacher if you let them.

Looking Over the Standards

You should be as familiar as possible with the Content Standards in your given subject area. That brings us to step 1 of the SCORE Process, Understanding of State Standards (Figure 3.1).

Figure 3.1 Step 1 of the SCORE Process:
Understanding of State Standards

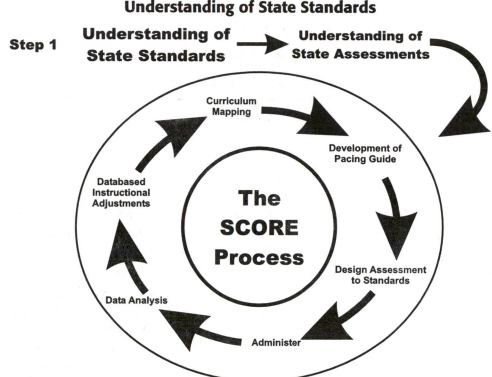

Every Content Standard has a noun and a verb in it. The best way to become familiar with the standards is to look for these. The noun indicates what skill is being taught. For example, let's say the standard reads like this:

Identify the setting in the selection.

The noun in this case is the word setting. Students are going to be learning about setting in some form or manner. Just as important, however, is the verb. The verb indicates exactly what the student needs to do with this skill and at what level. The verb in this case is identify, a lower-level skill. So identifying setting is what students need to be able to do. The expectation of this standard would be different if the standard were to read compare the setting. This is at a higher level of thinking and requires a different way of addressing the skill.

The verb ties in directly with the level of the learning on Bloom's taxonomy. As teachers, most of us are aware of Bloom's taxonomy and the structure of lower-level to higher-level thinking. Figure 3.2 is a graphic to refresh your memory.

Figure 3.2 Bloom's Taxonomy

Knowledge

Comprehension

Application

Analysis

Synthesis

Evaluation

The top three levels of Bloom's taxonomy are considered to be lower-level thinking. What is meant by that is that students do not have to go deep with their thought process in order to answer a question at this level. *Knowledge* is the most basic level, a simple recall of facts. If a teacher instructs you that Washington, DC is the nation's capital and you are able to memorize and answer that back when asked the same question, you have a knowledge-level skill. *Comprehension* involves the ability to read a passage and answer a question using the direct information contained within. For example if you read a passage that said, "Cole was a very tall man," and then were asked to physically describe the character of Cole, you would describe him as tall based on what the reading told you. *Application* is what we sometimes call the higher-level, lower-level thinking. Here students have to take something they know and apply it to a new situation. If students are taught how to add numbers, they should be able to take that skill and apply it to any two sets of numbers even if those particular numbers have not been covered in class.

Unfortunately, many tests in a traditional setting were written using lower-level questions. The regurgitation of facts set to rote memorization or reading tests where the answer can be found blatantly within the passage were common in classrooms. The current trend, however, is to push students to a higher level of thinking and have them go deeper into the content so they truly understand what it is they have learned. Content Standards are striving to get an enduring understanding of the skill so that students don't just memorize information for a test, write it down, and then forget about it. Rather students are being asked to understand the concept in many different ways, and in ways that will sustain their understanding for many years to come. These higher levels of thinking come in three categories.

Analysis is the first category and involves breaking down the information into parts and examining each part for an answer that is not obvious. Using the same example from before about the tall man, if it reads "Cole had to duck his head or risk hitting it on the top of the door," and the students are asked to describe Cole, they will still come to the conclusion that he was tall, having inferred it from the actions rather than simply being told. Analysis is typically looking at the larger picture, asking the why and how and not just the what, when, who, and where. It requires that students truly understand what they have read rather than hunting for a single key word.

Synthesis is the type of thinking that requires taking two different pieces of information and putting them together to make a completely different result. An example of this would be to take information from a graph about pollution statistics and reading an article about the affects of pollution, drawing a conclusion using the two.

Evaluation almost always involves using a judgment of some sort. What is important about this is that students provide not only their opinion, but can justify it based on a certain set of criteria, providing the why and how.

All three of these skills require that students put some thought into what they are doing, accessing the higher-level thinking skills of the brain. One thing that needs to be clear is that higher-level thinking does not necessarily mean it is more difficult. You could be asked who the 27th Vice President of the United States was. A difficult question no doubt, but a simple knowledge-based question (the answer by the way, in case you were wondering, is James Sherman). You can, however, ask a simple evaluation question such as do you like pizza and why. Typically, though, students do find higher-level questions to be more challenging.

Finding Key Verbs

You can use the verb of a Content Standard to identify in which level of Bloom's taxonomy it lies. Figure 3.3 is a chart that may help you to match the verb with the correct level of Bloom's taxonomy. *Bloom's Taxonomy Key Words* (p. 128) is a more comprehensive chart.

Figure 3.3 Chart of Verbs

Knowledge	choose, define, find, identify, locate, recall, recognize, select, show, tell
Comprehension	add, compare, describe, distinguish, explain, express, paraphrase, rephrase, summarize, understand
Application	answer, conduct, demonstrate, develop, illustrate, investigate, organize, present, produce, respond, solve
Analysis	classify, compare and contrast, deduce, distinguish, edit, examine, explain, infer, reason, validate
Synthesis	combine, compile, create, hypothesize, imagine, integrate, invent, organize, rearrange, revise
Evaluation	assess, conclude, criticize, debate, give opinion, justify, judge, prove, recommend, verify

Some of these terms will appear on more than one list, so keep in mind that just because the verb falls under a certain category does not mean it should be identified as thus. An example of this is the term *infer*. You can infer something simply by using comprehension. You can also infer by analysis. The question becomes which applies? That is why you must read the entire standard and understand the context of the verb.

The Taxonomy Table

A good way to organize the Content Standards is to place them in a Taxonomy Table. This requires going through each standard, identifying the verb, and using that verb to determine at which level on Bloom's taxonomy it falls. This work is very important because it lays the groundwork for all that follows. Using the *Taxonomy Table* (p. 129), place each content standard under one of Bloom's taxonomy levels. What this allows you to do is identify the minimum level of Bloom's taxonomy at which a question relating to this standard will be set. For instance, if the content standard reads:

Analyze problem situations involving proportional relationships and scale factors.

The verb obviously is *analyze* which puts the skill at a higher level. The noun is *proportional relationships and scale factors*. If as a teacher you were to only get students to identify or apply these skills, you will not have prepared them for that particular Content Standard. You have to take them one step further so that they have the ability to analyze the content.

Continue the taxonomy process by going through each and every Content Standard, paying close attention to the verbs and nouns, identifying where they would fall on Bloom's taxonomy. Keep in mind that this is a process and sometimes just looking at the verb alone will not give you the best determination of where it falls. You need to read the entire standard and take it in its context as to what it is that the student is being asked to know and do.

Consider the following Content Standard:

Identify and explain the sources of conflict that led to the American Revolution with emphasis on the perspectives of the Patriots, Loyalists, neutral colonists, and the British.

At first glance the first verb is *identify*, the lowest of Bloom's taxonomy levels, but delving deeper, we can see that there is much more going on in this standard. Students need to look at all the different perspectives and be able to explain why these groups all have varying points of view. There is going to be much deeper thinking going on with this standard than it seems.

In some cases there is a double verb to pay attention to that might elevate a level of Bloom's taxonomy to a higher one. Consider, for example, a standard that reads:

> Analyze important political values such as freedom, democracy, equality, and justice embodied in documents such as the Declaration of Independence, the United States Constitution, and the Bill of Rights, and defend their usefulness to governments around the world.

Notice the two verbs *analyze* and *defend*. The *analyze* verb clearly puts it at an analysis level but the added verb of *defend* pushes it up to an evaluation level. The lesson here is to not read the first verb you come across and put it at that level. Read the entire standard and make sure there are not additional verbs that are raising its level.

If possible it is better to go through the process of breaking down the standards according to Bloom's taxonomy with another colleague or group of colleagues so that discussion and debate about where the standard should be categorized can occur. One thing we always tell people when working on the Taxonomy Table is when in doubt, go to the higher level because students will have to be able to access the lower-level thinking first before they can move on and succeed at the higher level.

When placing the Content Standard on the chart, writing out each standard could become very tedious. Using a coding system that allows participants to use a small amount of space yet be easily referenced is recommended. Typically the subject area on the Taxonomy Table is broken into various topics found within each standard, which are different from state to state. An example of this would be the Content Standards for science in Wisconsin, which breaks down like this:

Science Connections

Nature of Science

Science Inquiry

Physical Science

Earth and Space Science

Life and Environmental Science

Science Applications

Science in Personal and Social Perspectives

These topics would be numbered or lettered (whatever your preference) in order so they would look like this:

A. Science Connections

B. Nature of Science

C. Science Inquiry

D. Physical Science

    E. Earth and Space Science

    F. Life and Environmental Science

    G. Science Applications

    H. Science in Personal and Social Perspectives

They could then easily be organized on the Taxonomy Table to look like Figure 3.4.

Figure 3.4 Taxonomy Table I

	Knowledge	Comprehension	Application	Analysis	Synthesis	Evaluation
A. Science Connections						
B. Nature of Science						
C. Science Inquiry						
D. Physical Science						
E. Earth and Space Science						
F. Life and Environmental Science						
G. Science Applications						
H. Science in Personal and Social Perspectives						

Typically, under each of these topics several specific skills or performance indicators are listed. Indicators fall under the topic and are usually numbered. Following the taxonomy process, each one of these would be examined with the verb underlined, putting it at a certain level of Bloom's taxonomy as shown in Figure 3.5.

Figure 3.5 Indicators with the Verb Underlined

A.   Science Connections

1.   *Develop* their understanding of the science themes by *using* the themes to *frame* questions about science-related issues and problems. (analysis)

2.   *Describe* limitations of science systems and *give reasons why* specific science themes are included in or excluded from those systems. (comprehension)

3.   *Defend* explanations and models by *collecting* and *organizing* evidence that supports them and *critique* explanations and models by *collecting* and *organizing* evidence that conflicts with them. (evaluation)

4.   *Collect* evidence to *show* that models developed as explanations for events were (and are) based on the evidence available to scientists at the time. (application)

5.   *Show* how models and explanations, based on systems, were changed as new evidence accumulated (the effects of constancy, evolution, change, and measurement should all be part of these explanations). (application)

6.   *Use* models and explanations to *predict* actions and events in the natural world. (synthesis)

7.   *Design* real or thought investigations to *test* the usefulness and limitations of a model. (synthesis)

8.   *Use* the themes of evolution, equilibrium, and energy to *predict* future events or changes in the natural world. (synthesis)

The indicators would then be placed on the Taxonomy Table as shown in Figure 3.6.

Figure 3.6 Taxonomy Table II

	Knowledge	Comprehension	Application	Analysis	Synthesis	Evaluation
A. Science Connections		2	4, 5	1	6, 7, 8	3

This would be done for all the standards until the Taxonomy Table is complete. This Taxonomy Table then acts as the foundation for every question written for a short-cycle assessment or any question asked in class. This table lets the teacher know exactly where the level of the question needs to be taught if the students are to be truly prepared to learn the Content Standard.

It is important that you keep your Taxonomy Table simple. If an entire staff of teachers is going through the SCORE Process, it is a good idea to decide as a group how you will code your standards so there will be consistency.

The Short of Understanding the Content Standards

By completing this process, teachers become more familiar with the Content Standards and realize at what level each one needs to be taught. By organizing them on the Taxonomy Table, the standards do not seem so overwhelming and give teachers a better idea how to teach them. It also provides a starting point for the short-cycle assessment development process and must be done with great diligence so that everything that follows is correct. If a builder has a poor foundation, no amount of work will make a good structure because no matter what is built, it will be on shaky ground and could fall down at any given moment. It is imperative to make sure your foundation is a solid one.

4

Understanding the State Assessments

A shocking occurrence ceases to be shocking when it occurs daily.

Alexander Chase

Why Worry About the Format of the Question?

When assessing a student and the knowledge and/or skills he or she know, you want to choose the method that will best display these attributes. You would not set up an assessment that would either trick the students into giving a false answer or that would not measure the skill. That is why it is important for students to be familiar with the format of the summative assessment their state gives. The more familiar they are, the more comfortable they will feel. After all, familiarity and practice breeds confidence.

That brings us to step 2 of the SCORE Process: Understanding State Assessments (Figure 4.1).

Figure 4.1 Step 2 of the SCORE Process: Understanding State Assessments

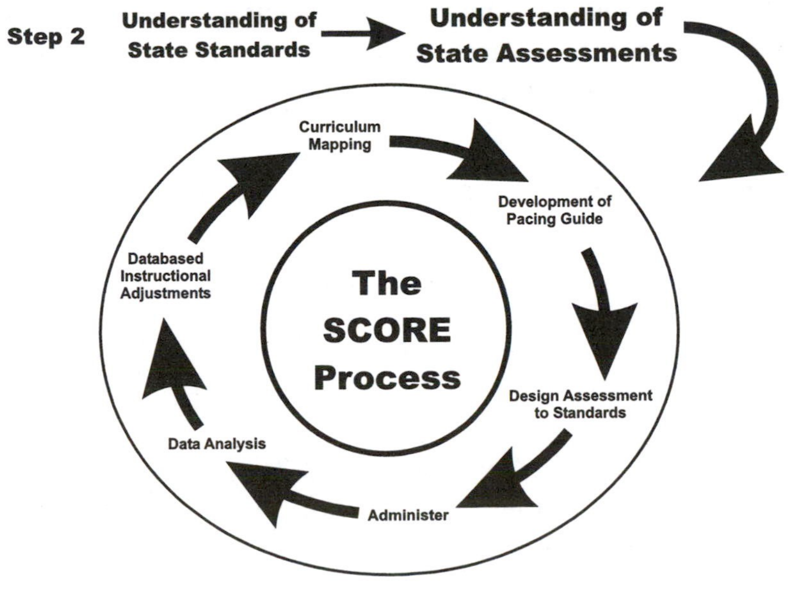

Different States, Different Formats

There is not a single common format that all state tests in our country follow. Some states, such as Tennessee and Oregon, give only multiple-choice questions, while others, such as Connecticut, include many constructed responses. Some, like Virginia, have constructed responses but maybe only on the writing portion of the test, while other states, such as Ohio, have them throughout all subjects. Some states, like Minnesota, have response grids for math or science problems where you figure out the answer and bubble it in on a grid. Most states have a longer section in their writing portion of the test which requires students to compose an essay from a writing prompt. Nebraska is one of the few states that allows its own districts to create tests and assess what the students know.

Each state test is unique unto itself but there are some similarities and patterns among them. The kinds of questions in this section are broken down into four types:

1. Multiple choice
2. Response grid
3. Constructed responses
4. Writing prompts

Review the section or sections that model your state test for help in getting students familiar with the formatting they will encounter when they are required to take the actual test.

Multiple-Choice Questions

Every state has multiple-choice questions on its assessment. A primary reason for this is that it makes it much easier to grade the hundreds and thousands of tests that students throughout the state take. Some states, such as Illinois, Pennsylvania, and California, have a simple four-choice, A–D, answer throughout the test, like this question from the Michigan science assessment:

A student receives an assignment to research and write a report on a nonrenewable resource of the Great Lakes region. Which of the following resources would be an appropriate choice?

A. fish
B. iron
C. trees
D. wind

Other states, such as Florida, Tennessee, and Texas, probably to break up the monotony or to ensure that a student has not skipped a question on accident, label their multiple-choice answer choices with consecutive letters. There are even some tests, like in Colorado, where letter choices are not provided at all. Correct bubbles are just filled in.

What is consistent is that there are always four choices. Some states such, as Ohio, provide only three choices to the students in the younger grades (grade 3 and below), but by the time the students take the summative assessment that determines whether or not they will graduate, there almost always are four choices.

Another consistency with most of the multiple-choice questions is that they do not use the phrases, "none of the above" or "all of the above" in their answer choices. The only exception to this is West Virginia in the math section where students were provided a fifth option, E, which read "none of these." Most assessments also do not use "both a and b" or "a and b but not c." Because of this, such possible answers should be eliminated from your classroom assessments. Students should be exposed to the formatting of the question they are likely to see on the state test.

With four possible answers of which only one is correct, the three incorrect choices are termed "distracters" because they could be the correct answer or are very close to it. In your classroom assessments you should not have any throwaway distracters or ones that the student can easily eliminate because they are silly responses or do not make any sense. The wrong answers should be thought through and distracters should represent what the student might put if they are rushing, not paying attention, or do not think the question through like they should. The idea is not to trick the students, but to ensure that they indeed have mastered the skill and can show that they have by eliminating possible answers and carefully reading each question.

Some multiple-choice questions use the phrase, "Which of the following is the *best* example of…" followed by four answers, all of which could be correct, but only one stands out as being the best. You might also see a question that uses the phrase, "Which of the following is *not* an example of…" and then three correct answer choices and one incorrect answer choice. This is a form of higher-level thinking because by eliminating, students have to analyze the question and the answer choices. You should try to incorporate questions like these into your daily classroom practice through assessments, daily practice, and verbal questioning with students.

Response Grid

Some states like Connecticut and Maryland provide students with a math or science response grids where they must figure out the math problem and bubble in the numerical answer. An example would be the Florida FCAT test, which has a response grid that looks like Figure 4.2.

Figure 4.2 Response Grid

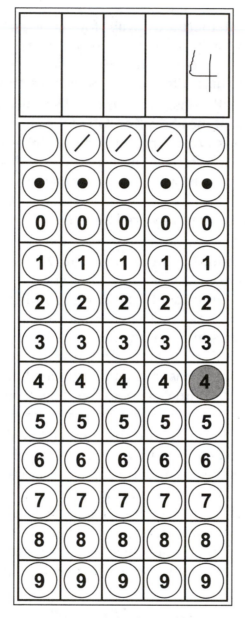

A teacher in a state test that uses response grids would better prepare students by including response grids not only on the short-cycle assessments, but also by having them on unit tests and daily problems. As you can see from Figure 4.2, it has spots to bubble in fraction bars or decimal points. Imagine how frustrating it would be to have a student calculate the correct answer and then bubble it in wrong because they did not have the experience of doing so before taking the test. Students need to become familiar with this format so that when they run across it on the test their first thought is, "Oh, these are just like the ones we use in the class."

Multipart Constructed Responses

Most state tests have short-answer questions that require some kind of written response. These questions can be straight forward questions or open-response questions that do not have a right or wrong answer. The question is designed to elicit a writing sample that shows the students' thought process and their ability to write. Typically these questions have several parts, consisting of multiple skills, so it is extremely important that your students begin to recognize this, break the question down into its various parts, and make sure they answer everything they need to. Sometimes these parts are made very obvious such as on the Rhode Island test:

a. A pyramid has a hexagon for its base. How many edges does the pyramid have?

b. A pyramid has a base that is a polygon with n sides. Use n to write an expression that represents the number of edges the pyramid has.

Some states do not make it so obvious. The breakdown of the question is vague as far as where the different parts are and students have to discern the parts for themselves. This is evidenced on the New Mexico science test as shown in Figure 4.3.

Figure 4.3 Sample Question from New Mexico Science Test

The diagram shows how water flowing from a reservoir is converted into electrical power for human use.

Hydropower Plant
Power Lines
Dam
Reservoir
Generator
Turbine
Water—Flow→
River

In your answer document, identify: 1 benefit and 1 disadvantage of using this type of technology to produce electricity.

Figure 4.3 is a two-part question, although not labeled clearly as such. One point is received for the advantage, the other point for the disadvantage. If the student does not recognize this, they might only give an advantage, thinking they have answered the question that was asked of them, when in fact the question asks for two different things.

Students also have the least amount of tolerance for these types of questions. They might give only a one- or two-word answer—or even worse, leave it blank. Students need to build an endurance to answer such questions so that they show the knowledge they have. (Remember the Endurance part of the "4 Es" in Chapter 1?) We have seen in many districts in which we have worked, students give very short responses or none at all on the first short-cycle assessment. By the second time, they have added a few more words here and there, and by the time they have been through the process a few times they are more comfortable in answering these types of questions and the format is no longer impeding their display of mastery.

This brings us to the rationale behind practicing in the classroom. If students are used to answering questions of these types of questions on daily or weekly assessments, or if you, as the teacher, phrase your verbal questions in two, three, or four parts, they will become familiar with looking for the various parts and making sure they answer each one of them.

At this point in the training process, teachers often share that their students will "sit there and refuse to answer" the constructed-response questions. If you have experienced this, ask yourself this question: "Do you believe that the students have all of the knowledge, expertise, and ability to answer the question, but are just being stubborn and refusing to try just to make a point?" Especially knowing and understanding the consequences of failing a graduation test? Now, look a little deeper into the cause and effect of this situation. Why would the student sit there and not try? Is it possible that they do not have any idea how to answer the question, and would rather not try than to lose face? Have you yourself ever been in a situation where you were faced with the same sort of dilemma? Imagine yourself in this situation: You are standing on the first tee of a professional golf course in the first round of a major golf tournament. You have played a little golf in the past, but have not practiced to the point of becoming proficient. Yet, here you are—ready to tee off in front of hundreds of people. What would you do? How high is your comfort level? Feel like not even trying? Your first impulse is probably to flee the golf course. What we know about human nature is that when people are uncomfortable, they either fight or flee. Similarly, that is what your students are doing when they "don't even try." They are fleeing. The difference is they are not actually leaving the room. To feel comfortable they need to feel prepared. To feel prepared they need practice. And most important, like a golf professional, they need a coach. Prepare to be the coach.

Writing Prompts

Most states have a writing assessment they give to students or include in the English Language Arts assessment. A writing prompt is just that—it prompts the student to give a lengthy written response. It usually is not evaluating specific skills such as literary terms or techniques. Instead, it is a general prompt that asks the students to pull from their own personal experience or juxtapose themselves in a situation.

The writing prompt is evaluated using a specific rubric that is very clear on what is and what is not an acceptable answer. Because so many states use rubrics to evaluate writing skills, students need to get used to what a rubric is and how they are used to evaluate writing. Whenever you have a writing session in class or use a writing prompt on an assessment, make students aware of the rubric. One way to do this is to have students use the rubric to evaluate themselves and others. Students should become familiar with how they are being evaluated so that they begin to recognize in their own writing what it is they need to include to get a favorable appraisal.

How to Help Students Become Comfortable with the Formatting

The best way to help students get comfortable with the formatting of the high-stakes test is to expose them to it as much as possible. This means to embed it in the daily practice of the classroom on tests and quizzes, homework assignments, daily problems, and even the way a teacher asks questions in class.

This also means eliminating formats students will not see on the state test. There are many formats that we as teachers have used over the years. Some of these include true and false items, matching items, sequencing items, and fill-in-the-blank items. Teachers have various reasons for using these different formats and they all have merit, but we recommend eliminating these items as much as possible and using only the formats the students will see on the high-stakes state test. Some teachers understandably become opposed to such an action, but the essential question that needs to be asked is: "What is the difference?" The purpose of an assessment is to assess whether the students understand the skill or not. What does it matter which format you use? This seems to run contrary to the argument made at the beginning of this chapter about the importance of consistency of format. The major difference is that each state has set a format it is going to use on every test it gives and this test is one with a lot at stake. Becoming familiar with the format is only going to work to the advantage of the student in doing well on the test. It is becoming a major responsibility of teachers to prepare students for the state test. To that degree, paying attention to the state test's format is invaluable.

The Short of Understanding the State Assessments

The more you use the formatting that the state test uses in the every day practices of the classroom, the better prepared your students are going to be for the high-stakes test. Familiarity with this formatting allows students to be more comfortable with the test and does not allow the set up to cause students to miss a question. Holding students back will be their ability, not their lack of comfort. If you are unsure of the format your state is using in testing, you can go to the your state's department of education and, in most states, access samples of tests or released tests from previous years. By just skimming through these, you can get a pretty good idea of the format your state uses. Be aware that different subject areas sometimes use different formats, so if you teach several subjects, be sure to check through them all. Remember that the idea is to expose the students to what they will see on the high-stakes test so they won't be surprised.

5

Creating a Pacing Guide

Science is organized knowledge. Wisdom is organized life.

Immanuel Kant

What is a Pacing Guide?

Now that you have become familiar with the Content Standards and organized them on the Taxonomy Table, you have to figure out how you are going to teach those standards over the course of the school year. Ideally, you must teach each standard. And not only do they all have to be taught, they have to be mastered so that if students learn something at the beginning of the year they have to have enough of an understanding of it to answer a question about it should it appear on a test at the end of the year. The best way to ensure that all of the standards will be taught and mastered is through the use of a pacing guide.

What is a pacing guide? The pacing guide is an organization of the standards that represents when you are going to teach and assess each of them. In essence, it is planning out the entire school year by deciding when students are going to learn each standard.

Why a Pacing Guide?

Why a pacing guide then? The obvious reason is that teachers should know when they are going to be teaching certain standards. There are many reasons for this. One might be because skills are building on one another and you have to introduce one standard before you lead to the next. The old adage of you can't run until you learn to walk applies here. Another reason is that it ensures no standards fall through the cracks or are simply not addressed. A pacing guide allows you to see the big picture, laying out the entire school year for your students and sets the pace of the learning (hence the name, pacing guide). That brings us to step 3 of the SCORE Process: Development of the Pacing Guide (Figure 5.1).

**Figure 5.1 Step 3 of the SCORE Process:
Development of the Pacing Guide**

There are some teachers who may see this as too limiting because they like to plan as they go along or they feel they need to see where their students are and then plan accordingly. Consider that the pacing guide is malleable, not set in stone. If there are a series of snow days or a lesson goes longer than expected because students explore it at a deeper level, the pacing guide is designed to be able to make adjustments.

When to Create a Pacing Guide

The best time to create a pacing guide is either at the very end of the school year for the next year, or a couple of weeks before the beginning of school. The rationale is very simple; the pacing guide needs to be created prior to the school year actually starting. By creating it prior to the school year, lesson plans can be designed with the Content Standards in mind. It also helps with the pacing of each grading period. Rather than bunch a majority of the standards into a single grading period, you can see the big picture and spread them out, making for a more natural learning process.

We mentioned before the concept of backwards building and how to create lessons with the end in mind. The pacing guide is what allows this to occur. The best case scenario is taking the pacing guide and creating the short-cycle assessment before even figuring out what lessons are to be taught. Once the assessment is in place the lessons can be created in order for the students to learn the skills they will need to know to answer these questions. Once all of this is rolled out backwards, teaching begins and students work on specific Content Standards that build off of one another. By the time the students take the short-cycle assessment that matches what was taught, the students are ready to show what they have learned.

How to Set Up a Pacing Guide

Many times the task of placing standards on a pacing guide is difficult for teachers. This is especially true in the subject of reading in the primary grades. The reason for this is that most of the time the teacher is continually teaching all of the standards all the time as reading is such an integrated process. The main purpose of the pacing guide with regard to short-cycle assessments is to divide up the standards into sections so that the short-cycle assessments can be developed. With that in mind, the following are the questions we ask the teachers to consider as they are placing the standards on the pacing guide:

♦ At what point do you want the information as to the student's progress in learning that particular standard?

♦ At what point would you expect the student to have "mastered" that standard?

♦ At what point would you begin to become concerned if that student had not "mastered" the standard?

♦ At what point would you feel it necessary to provide intervention for that standard?

Another thing to be very clear about when placing standards on the pacing guide is that instruction does not have to be limited to the grading period in which the standard is placed. For example, reading teachers will continue to teach inference throughout the entire year, but placement on the pacing guide will establish the point when the teachers feel they need data in order to make instructional decisions. Likewise, high school science teachers will continually instruct the scientific method, but at what point are they going to provide intervention for those students who are still not clear about its use? Interpretation of maps and diagrams in a middle school social studies class will be used all school year, but at what point are the students expected to have "mastered" that skill?

Something you do not want to do is include every content standard multiple times on the pacing guide because then the short-cycle assessments will be too long. Spreading the Content Standards throughout the year will make the short-cycle assessments more manageable for students and thus help to increase their test-taking stamina. Undoubtedly there will be those standards you consider to be of such great value that you might want to assess them on more than one short-cycle assessment just to be sure mastery has occurred and been maintained. There may also be questions on which students do not perform well. This may lead to a standard needing to be retaught, and therefore moved (sometimes temporarily) on the pacing guide. Sometimes as a result of unforeseen circumstances such as snow days, too many assemblies, or just a shortened grading period, some standards are unable to be taught within the designated time on the pacing guide. Obviously the students are not going to show mastery on the assessment if this occurs. You might have to place another question that addresses this Content Standard on the next short-cycle assessment, and, again, you may choose to temporarily place the standard on the next grading period.

Your pacing guide should have as many divisions in it as the amount of short-cycle assessments you are going to give. If using the *Figuring Out Which SCORE Model Works Best for You* (p. 126) reveals you are going to have four short-cycle assessments, you should have an equal number of divisions in your pacing guide. If you are going to give a pre- and a postassessment for the grading period, you would use the same content standards for both assessments, but not the same questions. If your school has decided to have only two short-cycle assessments, the pacing guide would be divided into two sections. Use the blank *Curriculum Pacing Guide for the SCORE Process* (p. 130) to layout your pacing guide.

Also consider setting up your pacing guide according to when the high-stakes test is given to your students. If the test is administered in March and many of the important Content Standards that may be present on that test are listed in the last grading period after that assessment has been given, then your students may not be as prepared as you would like. In this case, you may need to front load the more important standards in the first part of the year to ensure that students know them in time for the state assessment. Subsequently, you may want to save some of the standards you consider to be either review or a continuation of something already mastered until the end of the year on the pacing guide. If your state gives the assessment in the fall, as some do, you will want to place those Content Standards you have determined to be important standards at the beginning of the year or at the end of the year for the previous grade so they are fresh in the students' minds.

Coding the Pacing Guide

When putting the pacing guide together you do not want to have to write out every Content Standard word for word. We try to make the pacing guide one sheet of paper that acts as a reference. As a result, we use the method for coding the Content Standards, which was mentioned in Chapter 3. The standard is numbered or lettered even if it isn't already done by the state, and then the indicator underneath is also numbered.

You would place these coded Content Standards into the pacing guide so that you can look at everything on a single page. Figure 5.2 is an example pacing guide for 10th grade Math.

Figure 5.2 Sample Pacing Guide for 10th Grade Math

Grading Period 1 Math Content Standards	Grading Period 2 Math Content Standards	Grading Period 3 Math Content Standards	Grading Period 4 Math Content Standards
1–1	3–3	1–2	3–1a
2–5	3–10	1–3	3–1 c
3–1 a,b,d	4–3	1–4	3–3 b
3–2	4–5	2–1	3–3 d
3–3 a	4–6	2–2	3–4
5–1	4–7	2–3	3–5
5–2	4–8	2–4	3–6
	4–9	4–1	3–7
	4–10	4–2	3–8
	4–11		3–9
	4–12		4–4
			5–3
			5–4
			5–5
			5–6
			5–7
			5–8

How much detail used on the pacing guide is up to the individual teacher as long as they can understand it and read it. Some teachers like to include descriptors to help remind them what skills the Content Standards are covering. Figure 5.3 is an example of a 9th grade English pacing guide.

Figure 5.3 Sample 9th Grade English Pacing Guide

English 1	English 2	English 3
2–3 (infer meaning)	2–2 (responses to lit.)	2–1 (define words/context clues)
3–1 (reading comprehension)	2–3 (infer meaning)	2–5 (Greek/Latin roots)
3–3 (adjusting speed)	2–5 (Greek/Latin roots)	4–1 (rhetorical devices)
5–3 (conflict)	4–1 (organizational patterns)	4–4 (propaganda/bias)
5–6 (genre)	4–4 (propaganda/bias)	5–2 (setting)
6–3 (thesis statement)	4–7 (public documents)	5–8 (point of view/mood & tone)
6–8 (topic sentences)	5–1 (direct/indirect characterization)	6–3 (thesis statement)
6–6 (intro/body/conclusion)	5–4 (universal themes)	6–4 (purpose/audience)
6–9 (language)	5–7 (irony)	7–4 (research paper)
6–11 (clarity of writing)	5–8 (point of view)	8–4 (parallel structure)
6–12 (add/delete details)	5–9 (symbols)	
7–2 (responses to lit.)	6–13 (rearrange)	
7–5 (persuasive comp.)	6–15 (proofread)	
8–1 (spelling)	6–16 (apply tools to judge)	
8–2 (cap./punc.)		

How to Use the Pacing Guide

Once the pacing guide is created it will be used along with the Taxonomy Table to develop the short-cycle assessments. You simply begin with your first section of the pacing guide and write questions for each standard listed. You want to use the Taxonomy Table to determine at what level you will be writing the question as well as the format of the question. This will be explained in more detail in Chapters 6 and 7. You will write as many questions as you have Content Standards. Sometimes you may want to write more than a single question per standard. For instance, consider the following content standard from the Washington State Essential Academic Learning Requirements for History:

> Understand events, trends, individuals, and movements shaping United States, world, and Washington State history.

This particular standard could cover a lot of material. Think about it, movements that shape the United States, world, and Washington State history easily could be more than a thousand events. How do you develop a single question that covers this Content Standard? You may have to write several questions to address a single standard. Other times a standard may clearly have two parts. An example of this is seen in this standard from the Kansas State Curricular Standards of 8th Grade Reading:

> Identifies the use of literary devices (e.g., *foreshadowing, flashback, figurative language, imagery, symbolism*) in a text and explains how the author uses such devices to help establish *tone* and *mood*.

There are two skills going on here, the first being able to identify the literary device in the first place, and second explaining the idea of tone and mood. It would be difficult to capture the entire standard in a single question, so you might break this standard into a couple of questions.

The pacing guide should act as a blueprint for the writing of the assessment for that grading period. The Content Standards you have included on your pacing guide for that grading period should have a corresponding question or questions on your short-cycle assessment, thus ensuring that there is at least one question for every standard.

The Short of the Pacing Guide

The pacing guide should lay out the entire school year for the teacher, indicating which Content Standard will be assessed in which grading period. Using this guide, the short-cycle assessment will be developed, using the Taxonomy Table created in Chapter 3 to determine at what level the question should be written. How the pacing guide is set up is up to the individual teacher, school, or district, and how it will work best for each.

Keep in mind that the pacing guide is not set in stone and can be changed to adjust to the pace of the class or for the inevitable hiccups that occur throughout the course of the school year. Just make sure all the Content Standards you want and need to cover are taught.

6

Question Writing: Constructing Questions that Address the Standard

It is not the answer that enlightens, but the question.

Decouvertes

This chapter walks you through the steps of how to write questions for your short-cycle assessment. The design of your assessment—the number of questions or how many of each format—is addressed in Chapter 7.

Why Write the Questions Myself?

The question we probably get asked the most when working with schools is "Why should I write the questions myself?" More often than not teachers want us to simply give them the questions or allow them to use ones from a workbook. There are many fine books that have great questions, but we feel this defeats the purpose of the process, which is to improve classroom instruction. If we just give teachers a set of well-written questions will that cause teachers to improve their own question-writing ability? That would be like a person who wants to learn how to make furniture just being given a finished piece of woodwork. Much like the real furniture maker, these questions must be handcrafted and shaped so that the pieces fit together and the end result is that the teachers are better at asking questions. This directly benefits the students.

One of the most difficult discussions we have when working with teachers is that they all think they are already great question writers. After all, they have been teaching and making assessments for years. We can tell you that after having learned to write higher-level questions ourselves, when we went back to our own classroom assessments (the ones we thought were so well written) we were embarrassed at what we found. Further analysis revealed them to not be well written and many times they did not measure the skill we intended to measure. Even tests that were designed for gifted students had few higher-level thinking skills with most of the questions requiring only a rote memorization of facts. We realized that being a good question writer is not something that just happens. You have to purposely work at it.

Think about your own training to become a teacher. How much time was spent teaching you how to write questions or how to ask quality questions in class? Were there any courses on how to write assessments, or like most things in teaching, were you simply thrown into the deep end of the pool and told to sink or swim? If your experience is anything like ours, very little training was given in the art of writing questions. That is why it is important to check your ego at the door and enter this part of the process with an open mind.

You truly might already be very good at writing questions and it is not our place to determine whether you are or not, but what we show you in this chapter will help you to write better questions that measure the skill it intends to using the different levels of Bloom's taxonomy. By going through this process you will become much better not only at writing the questions, but asking them in your day-to-day practice as you look for higher-level thinking skills from your students.

How to Determine What Level of Question and What Format of Question

The first consideration when writing a question is determining what level of Bloom's taxonomy the particular standard is at. This should already be done if you have taken to time to look over the standards carefully and created your Taxonomy Table. If you skipped step 1 of the SCORE Process we encourage you to go back and lay down this important groundwork. This process, which seems to some like a waste of time, actually saves you a lot of time in the long run. Whenever you have to write a question you simply draw on the Taxonomy Table to determine which level will be the minimum for the question.

The second consideration is the format of the question. The format should reflect the format of your state assessment. If your state assessment is one that has all multiple-choice questions, your short-cycle assessment should reflect this and all the questions should be multiple-choice. However, if there are constructed response questions or writing prompts, you should consider those as well, and include them in your assessment. The analysis of the state assessment in step 2 of the SCORE Process will help you figure this out.

Many times the standard itself will determine the format of the question. For instance, if the standard reads like this:

> Show that when elements are listed in order according to the number of protons (called the atomic number) the repeating patterns of physical and chemical properties identify families of elements.

The verb *show* indicates that students should be doing something more than just choosing an answer in a multiple-choice question. The standard is asking the students to show you so the format is more conducive to a constructed response where an explanation or creation of a chart or diagram is possible. There are certain verbs that will clue you into the choice of the format. Here is a list of verbs that lend themselves to constructed response questions:

- Show
- Demonstrate
- Describe
- Express
- Illustrate
- Examine
- Create
- Invent
- Criticize
- Debate
- Judge

Keep in mind that just because a verb appears on this list does not mean you cannot write a multiple-choice question for it.

Writing the Questions

Now that you have determined the level and format you can begin to write the question. The easiest way to write a question is simply to take the statement that is the standard and turn it into a question. For example, if the standard reads:

Compare and order the relative size of common U.S. customary units and metric units; e.g., mile and kilometer, gallon and liter, pound and kilogram.

It could become a question with the addition of just a few simple words:

How would you compare and order the relative size of common U.S. customary units and metric units; e.g., mile and kilometer, gallon and liter, pound and kilogram?

Voila! You have the basis for a very good question that certainly covers the standard because it is the standard. Now if it were this easy you would not need this book, but this is the jumping off point. You can turn this backbone of a question into a two-part constructed response:

Part A: How would you compare the relative size of common U.S. customary units such as foot, yard, inch, mile to its metric unit counterparts; e.g., mile and kilometer, gallon and liter, pound and kilogram?

Part B: Place the units of measure, U.S. and metric, in their proper order from largest to smallest.

Or a multiple-choice question:

Which is the *best* way to compare the relative size of common U.S. units to its metric unit counterparts?

a.	mile	foot	inch
	kilometer	meter	centimeter
b.	mile	yard	inch
	kilometer	centimeter	millimeter
c.	mile	yard	inch
	kilogram	centimeter	milligram
d.	mile	yard	inch
	kilometer	meter	centimeter

Changing the standard itself into a question allows you to see how it can be broken down even further and is a great place to start. You can try doing this with a couple of the standards you will be working with using the *Standard to Question* (p. 131) activity.

Using the Language of the Standard

Many times when writing questions teachers will complain that if they use the verb of the standard in their question, students will not understand the question. The words used in the standard are too difficult for the students to comprehend. An example of this is shown in the following standard:

Determine the setting of the story.

Teachers understandably want to make this easier for their students who might not know the meaning of the word "determine" by changing the question to:

What is the setting of the story?

No harm no foul, right? The question is essentially the same, just easier to understand. The question we pose to teachers who bring up this very valid point is: "Would you rather your students not be familiar with the term on your short-cycle assessment, or later on when it is used on the high-stakes test?" The state is probably going to use the same verb in the question that the standard uses. If you truly want to prepare students for this you need to familiarize them with the state's vocabulary by using it on your short-cycle assessments, weekly assessments, and daily classroom vocabulary.

Writing a Constructed Response Question

Typically the easiest question to write is the constructed response so we will start with it. The reason it is the easiest is that you can write the question without having to worry about fitting the answer into a structured multiple-choice format. However, you do need to consider that the constructed response question needs to be clearly formatted as to the number of parts required. In other words, if you are writing a two-point question, the question has to have two clear parts to it. If it is a four-point question, it needs to have four clear parts. A single question should not be worth four points. Each part must be worth a single point.

No matter what format the question takes, when dealing with a multipart question we recommend that you do not phrase a question like this and consider it four parts:

> What are four reasons the Colonists declared independence from the British before the start of the American Revolution?

Yes, it is true that this would easily break down into four points, one for each correct answer, but it is only measuring a single skill. A four-point question should have four separate skills to it. That way, you will gain more information about your students' proficiency of that skill. After all, if a student earns two of the four points on the question, what does that tell you? That is only 50%. Did the student really understand the American Revolution, or was the student just reciting back a memorized fact? Keeping in mind the importance of assessing four different skills, the question would look more like this:

> What are two major reasons the Colonists declared independence from the British before the start of the American Revolution? (1 skill, 2 reasons) Do you think these reasons were valid (make sure to explain your answer)? (1 skill) How might someone who was a Loyalist (still loyal to the crown) see these reasons? (1 skill) How might things be different if the Revolutionaries had not been able to convince enough of the Colonists they were being treated poorly? (1 skill)

There are clearly four different skills addressed here, expanding the original question. The first question asks for two major reasons and would actually only be worth a single point. Because the skill is to provide reasons the student would have to provide two correct reasons to receive the point (on state assessments there is no such thing as a half point). The second skill asks the student to state an opinion but makes sure to have students explain their answer. If the question had simply read "Do you think these reasons were valid?," technically the student could have just answered yes or no and received credit. If you want the student to provide detail or an explanation, you need to specifically ask for that in the question. Do not just assume. There are also some higher-level questions included here to assess whether the student truly understands the origins of the American Revolution. One asks the student to assume the role of a Loyalist, giving an answer from a different perspective. This is an analysis question. The final question requires the student to suppose something happened that did not. Although there is no right or wrong answer, students would have to explain their rationale in order to receive the point for the question. This entire question measures the same information as the first one but at many different levels.

Another consideration when writing a constructed response question is that this is the perfect opportunity to integrate those graphic organizers that state assessments are so fond of using. For example, examine the two-part constructed response question used earlier in this chapter:

> Part A: How would you compare the relative size of common U.S. customary units such as foot, yard, inch, mile to its metric unit counterparts; e.g., mile and kilometer, gallon and liter, pound and kilogram?
>
> Part B: Place the units of measure, U.S. and metric, in their proper order from largest to smallest.

This question lends itself very well to a couple of graphic organizers. Part A could require the students to fill in a compare-and-contrast chart such as a Venn Diagram (Figure 6.1). Part B could ask the students to complete a largest-to-smallest chart (Figure 6.2). Notice how this question changes when using graphic organizers.

Figures 6.1 Part A: Compare-and-Contrast Chart: Venn Diagram

Part A: Complete the Venn Diagram below comparing the relative size of a common US customary unit to its metric unit counterpart.

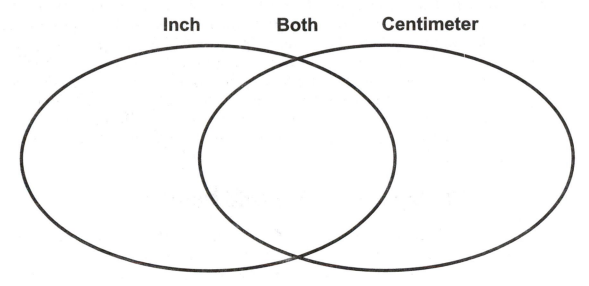

Figure 6.2 Part B: Largest-to-Smallest Chart

Part B: Place the following units of measure, US and metric, in their proper order from largest to smallest by filing out the chart below. Units: inch, kilometer, yard, millimeter.

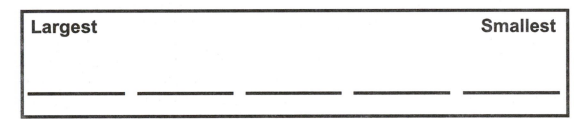

An advantage of using graphic organizers whenever you can is that the students will get used to seeing a question in different forms. It lets students know constructed response questions do not have to be presented only in words.

Constructed response questions are good for higher-level standards because typically it is much easier to write a higher-level constructed response question than a higher-level multiple-choice question. Remember that when writing a constructed response question that only one of the parts needs to be at a higher level for the entire question to be considered higher level. In the American Revolution example used previously, the first skill is simply lower level recall. The next question is at an application level, using the facts to back up choices. The third question requires analysis, asking the student to take the knowledge they have and extrapolate it to a specific point of view. Finally, the last question involves synthesis where the student has to take the argument apart and put it back together in the form of a different argument showing how history would be different. The question continues to build upon itself the more it proceeds. This is a good way to construct a multipart question—start with a lower-level question and work your way up to the higher level. This "primes the pump," so to speak, for students, taking their lower-level knowledge and having them expand upon it in higher-level critical thinking form. Setting the question up like this can also give students the confidence they need to answer constructed response questions because the lower-level questions typically are easier. Students attempt the first part, finding it is easy to answer, and move on to the next part of the question with the self-assurance they need to make them willing to answer the remainder of the question.

Writing a Response Grid Question

Some states have response grid answer sheets for their math or science problems. The rationale for this is that students will have to provide the correct answer rather than having a number of possible choices. The students calculate the correct numerical answer and then fill in the appropriate bubbles on the response grid.

If you teach in a state in which your assessment does not have response grids you might be tempted to skip this section of this chapter. We ask that you continue reading because this section also includes information on how to write math questions at a higher level—which is tricky in and of itself.

Response grid questions, just like other questions, need to be written at the correct level of Bloom's taxonomy even though at first glance they may seem to be straightforward application questions of studying a problem and figuring it out. There are ways to write higher-level questions that come to a single correct answer. For example, to write an analysis-level math question, you simply have to pose the problem as a word problem where the student has to break down a concept or idea into parts and show relationships among the parts. Figure 6.3 is an example of an analysis math question.

Figure 6.3 Analysis Math Question

The tables show some bowling scores. A higher number indicates a better score.

Dave's Scores			Bill's Scores	
152	138		210	105
138	141		105	105
141	141		118	118
144	144		131	131
141	152		105	210
158	158		215	215

How much would the person with the lower average have to improve his game in order to be better than the person with the higher average?

Obviously there is a lot of analyzing going on here. The student will first figure out the average of both bowlers, then figure out how much less one is than the other, and then figure out how much better he would have to bowl to be higher than the bowler with the higher average.

For a synthesis question, the student has to bring together parts to form a new whole. This can be taking information from a written passage and a chart to create a new whole, or taking information from a graph and a formula to create a new whole. The pattern is that the information needed to solve the problem comes from two different sources. Figure 6.4 is an example of a synthesis math problem.

Figure 6.4 Synthesis Math Problem

You work a different number of hours each day. The table shows your total pay (P) and the number of hours (H) you worked. Here is a model that relates the dependent variables P in terms of the independent variable H ($P = 6H$). If you work 6 hours on the fifth day, what will your total pay be?

Total pay, P	$18	$42	$48	$30
Hours worked, H	3	7	8	5

This question is at a synthesis level because students must take the information from the paragraph, namely the formula it provides, combine it with information contained within the table, and then come up with the new answer of $36, which they would then bubble in on their response grid.

Evaluation is having to make a judgment. In math this can be complicated, because a judgment usually involves opinion whereas many times math is a right or wrong proposition. There is no debating the fact that $2 + 2 = 4$. It is always going to equal 4. However, evaluation can be done using mathematics. Figure 6.5 is an example of an evaluation question for math.

Figure 6.5 Math Evaluation Question

Suppose 400 M&M's fit into a can of pop.

Judge which of the following would most likely be how many M&M's would fit in a gallon (64 ounces) milk jug.

7130, 800, 5000, 20000, 1200, 2200, 3500, 12500, 600, 10000

Here students are given information with which they must make a judgment that is not an exact answer but one that could be close to the probable solution. There are also several possible choices, causing students to have to eliminate more than the usual three distracters of a multiple-choice question. The students will need to examine many different parts before coming up with the correct answer of 2200 using their judgment.

No matter what level of question you write for a response grid it is important that your students know how to fill it out correctly. Be sure to give your students practice on responding to questions using grids in class and on the short-cycle assessments. You can practice writing a response grid question by using the *Response Grid Question Practice* (p. 132).

Writing Prompts for Longer Responses

Many states have a writing assessment that requires students to compose longer writing samples than required on the constructed response questions. These writing prompts typically do not require students to display any knowledge-based information. Instead they are designed to see how good a writer the students are, asking them to share a life experience, having to persuade the reader to their opinion, or making a judgment and backing that up. Here are some examples of typical written response prompts:

- ◆ Your school asks you to nominate a Best Teacher Award. You must nominate a teacher and explain why you think he or she deserves such an honor.

- ◆ Write a composition about something special you have done.

- ◆ If there is something you could change in the world, what would it be and why would you make this change?

- ◆ Your school is creating a time capsule. What three things would you include in the capsule and why would you choose these items?

♦ You have been given a million dollars to spend as you like. Write about how you would spend it.

When choosing a prompt you have to decide what sort of writing you wish the students to display. Will it be a narrative, descriptive, or persuasive piece of writing? Some states, such as Nebraska, have specific categories of writing at different grade levels. Make sure to check your state assessment to see if it follows a pattern such as this.

When writing your own writing prompts it is important not to use anything you have already been working on in class. For instance, if you have been talking a great deal about ancestry and practicing writing samples in class using this prompt, you do not want to have a prompt similar to this on your short-cycle assessment. The reason for this is that the students have had too much preparation on this topic. Consequently, they will have no trouble structuring their response because you worked on it as a class. This tends to make the student response a knowledge-level response—or remembering what was worked on in class. When the actual prompt appears on the state assessment there will have been no preparation work and students will have to create their writing for themselves. You need to get them used to this process by providing prompts they are unfamiliar with.

When determining how to evaluate the written response try to use the same rubric the state uses for its test—and don't be afraid to share the rubric with your students. The more you make students familiar with this rubric the more they will be aware of the expectations the state has for them when taking the high-stakes assessment. If you wish to look at sample rubrics or create your own, *Writing Your Own Rubric* (p. 134) is an activity to make a basic rubric for writing assessments that you can check against example rubrics in *Alaska's 6-Point Rubric* (p. 135), not to mention *Blank Rubrics* (p.136).

Writing a Multiple-Choice Question

Even though this is the format of question you will use the most, we decided to talk about it last because if you understand how to write the constructed response questions you essentially already know how to write the multiple-choice questions. We are going to show you how to write a good multiple-choice question using a single standard and writing a question on each level of Bloom's taxonomy. We will also provide keys to writing on those various levels. We will use an English standard:

Identify the literary term *foreshadowing*.

In this form, the logical question to write is a knowledge-level question because the verb *identify* is a key word for knowledge. Using our technique, we will turn the standard into a constructed response question, making sure to use the same verb so that students become familiar with it.

Identify what foreshadowing is.

Now that we have it in the form of a constructed response question we turn in into a multiple-choice question simply by providing some possible answers students might give to a constructed response. Remember, the incorrect answers need to act as distracters, providing possibilities a student could think were the correct response if they did not actually know the answer. Here is what a knowledge-level multiple-choice question would look like:

Identify what foreshadowing is.

  a. An act of providing vague advance indications

  b. Going back in time to revisit a scene

  c. Providing a surprise climax to the story

  d. Predicting what will occur in a story

The distracters are all legitimate if the students were simply taking the term and trying to infer its meaning. They have to know its definition in order to select the correct answer.

Comprehension usually involves the student being given the information in a reading passage and then showing that they understand the information. One thing we always try to encourage is the inclusion of reading passages, even on the math, science, and social studies assessments. They appear on the state assessments in all the subject areas and they also improve the reading comprehension of students, which is valuable in any subject. A multiple-choice comprehension question would look like this:

Foreshadowing: the technique of giving clues to coming events in a narrative.

Using the above definition, when do you think foreshadowing would be most effectively used?

  a. at the beginning of a story

  b. at the climax of a story

  c. at the falling action of a story

  d. at the end of a story

Notice the definition is given in this case but the student still has to comprehend the use of foreshadowing, taking it a step further and indicating when it would most likely appear. Even though the answer is not given verbatim, it can be implied through the context clue given in the definition of *coming events* which would make the answer at the beginning of the story.

The idea of application is taking the knowledge that you have and applying it to a situation. It is sort of like the idea of putting the concept into practice. The following question is an example of application:

> From the above excerpt, identify which of the following is an example of foreshadowing.
>
> a. Angie brags that she has never been sick before.
> b. Angie goes out in the rain and catches pneumonia.
> c. Angie's father remembers a time he fought pneumonia.
> d. Angie dies and she is laid to rest in the very grave she had been chucking rocks into at the beginning of the story.

Although an excerpt is not provided you can get the idea of the student having to identify which section of the story would be described as foreshadowing. They have to take their knowledge of what foreshadowing is and apply it to the situation.

Analysis is breaking the concept down into parts. In this example of an analysis question…

> Looking at the following passage, characterize which technique is best displayed by the author.
>
> a. foreshadowing
> b. flashback
> c. parallel plots
> d. tone

…the student not only has to apply the knowledge to the situation, the student must eliminate the other techniques, analyzing the passage for the correct one. By eliminating, the student is thinking at a higher level by breaking information down and looking at the different parts. The key to writing an analysis question is to set up the question so that it leads to a single answer through a logical progression. One way to think of it is that the student must explain his or her answer rather than just give it to you.

That takes us to synthesis. As stated before, synthesis is bringing together parts to make a different whole. The events listed are not included in the passage. Here is the foreshadowing standard with a synthesis question:

> Examining the incomplete passage above, speculate about which event would most likely occur if the author is using foreshadowing.
>
> a. Jake will drop the ball.
> b. Jake will hit a home run.

    c. Jake's team will lose the game.

    d. Jake will wake up and it will all be a dream.

Foreshadowing leads the student to speculate what will likely happen, but the student has to take the actions in the story and combine those actions with their knowledge of what foreshadowing is. Synthesis questions typically arrive at new endings.

    Finally the evaluation level requires a judgment of some sort. The problem with this level in regard to multiple-choice questions is how can a student provide an opinion if they are simply choosing an answer already provided to them—it is their opinion so how could what the student chooses be marked wrong? The way to effectively write an evaluation question is to put the student in the shoes of someone else or put them in a scenario where the requirements behind the judgment are laid out for them so that there would be a logical choice for the opinion. For instance, in this evaluation question…

> Imagine you are writing a mystery novel. Judge which of the following literary techniques you would use to best create suspense.
>
>   a. falling climax
>
>   b. foreshadowing
>
>   c. parallel plots
>
>   d. flashback

…the question lays out the requirements of the decision, which is a mystery novel and the creation of suspense. Even though it is a judgment, these requirements point the student in the direction of foreshadowing because it is the one technique that would most likely create suspense in a mystery novel.

    There are a couple of additional tips about writing multiple-choice questions. One thing to remember is that the answers you provide do not need to be one word answers. If you are asking a higher-level question in the form of a constructed response it would require four sentence answers for the students to choose from. Here is what it would look like:

> What was the most likely result of the government's deregulation of local telephone service?
>
>   a. Local phone service prices increased because fewer people had access to the service.
>
>   b. Local phone service prices increased because regulation had artificially kept rates low.
>
>   c. Local phone service prices decreased because deregulation resulted in increased competition.

    d. Local phone service prices decreased because companies were able to use cable television lines.

The answers are more than short responses; they are explanations in sentence form. Answers can even be longer, requiring students to choose the constructed response they would have written had they been required to write one.

Also remember that just because the verb of a higher-level question has been used, the question is not necessarily a higher-level question. For example, the question:

    Evaluate what 4 + 4 equals.

…is clearly not an evaluation question even though the verb evaluate was used. This is an application question. Make sure the verb in your question truly does perform at the level it indicates.

Remember that multiple-choice questions do not even have to have a written answer at all. If you have a science question concerning a graphic it might look something like this:

Which of these represents a strike-slip fault?

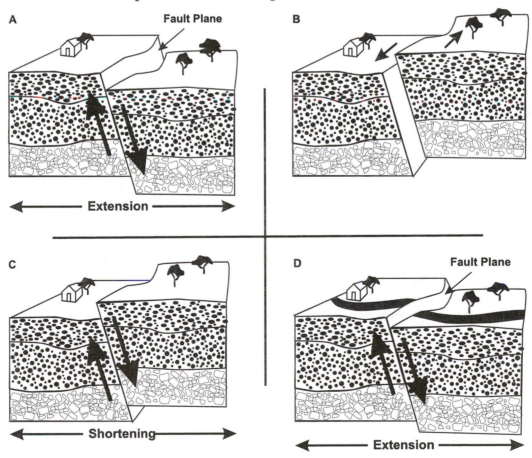

Hopefully this gives you a good idea how to write a question at the correct level. For some people it helps to see what not to do. *What Not to Write* (p. 138) shows common mistakes people make and how to avoid them. *Goldilocks and the Six Levels of Bloom's Taxonomy* (p. 141) is a question writing activity. Following that is a template, *How to Write a Multiple-choice Question* (p. 145). We highly recommend you do these activities before tackling your own assessment using your pacing guide and its standards; the practice of writing the questions and seeing them in a simple form will help you.

Writing Questions for Difficult Standards

Teachers often ask whether there can be a question written for every standard. You have to be creative, but every single Content Standard can be measured with a question, even the ones that seem to be a classroom skill or performance-based. Here are some of the more common skills from various subjects that pose a challenge in writing a question:

English

Independently read books for various purposes (e.g., for enjoyment, for literary experience, to gain information or to perform a task).

Monitor your own comprehension by adjusting speed to fit the purpose, or by skimming, scanning, reading on, looking back, note taking, or summarizing what has been read so far in text.

Math

Conduct simple probability experiments, e.g., rolling number cubes or drawing marbles from a bag.

Determine appropriate data to be collected to answer questions posed by students or the teacher, collect and display data, and clearly communicate findings.

Social Studies

Demonstrate effective citizenship traits.

Work effectively to achieve group goals.

Science

Choose the appropriate tools or instruments and use relevant safety procedures to complete scientific investigations.

Develop oral presentations using clear language, accurate data, appropriate graphs, tables, maps, and available technology.

The best way to set up such demonstration skills in a paper-and-pencil assessment question is the use of a scenario. This involves putting the student in a second-person situation and having them react, or making it a third-person situation and having them determine how the person should react. Here is a second-person example using the group work standard from social studies:

> You are a member of a group. You have to create a presentation on how a volcano works. Which of the following scenarios would *best* help you achieve this group goal?
>
> a. Divide up the tasks based upon equality
>
> b. Divide up tasks based on the strengths of the group members
>
> c. Divide up the tasks based on how smart the members are
>
> d. Divide up the tasks based on the availability of each member to work outside of class

Notice how the student is in the shoes of the person who must make a decision given a certain criteria. Although not as good as actually demonstrating it in the classroom, it is the next best thing.

Here is a third-person example using a performance English standard:

> Jake has been assigned to conduct research for a paper on Abraham Lincoln. Which of the following methods would be the *best* way for Jake to monitor his own comprehension?
>
> a. skimming
>
> b. reading on
>
> c. scanning
>
> d. summarizing

Not only does this make the student decide what to do in the scenario it also covers all aspects of the standard with the distracters students must eliminate.

These are just a couple of ways to maneuver your way around difficult standards. Much like your students in their exposure to the assessments, the more you expose yourself to writing questions the better you will become at figuring out how to write higher level and difficult questions. Practicing will allow question writing to become part of your skill set, transferring to the work you prepare for your students in the classroom and your discussion questions as well.

The Short of Writing Questions

When writing questions for your short-cycle assessment there are some things to consider. The level of the question in regard to Bloom's taxonomy will be determined by the verb the standard uses. This should have been plotted on your Taxonomy Table, which you completed in Chapter 3. Remember to use the vocabulary from the standard as the vocabulary in your question whenever possible.

The decision of using only multiple-choice questions, a mix of multiple-choice and constructed response questions, or any other decision having to do with the format of the questions should be determined by the format of your state assessment. Your state's assessment was analyzed in Chapter 4. Your short-cycle assessment should match it so that you are getting students ready for the atate assessment. The actual standards you cover in your short-cycle assessment are determined by the pacing guide you created in Chapter 5.

It is important to practice how to write different formats and different levels of questions in order to learn how to write effective questions. Question writing, like anything else, is a learned skill. Although you might think you are already quite accomplished at this, accept this challenge to practice writing multiple-choice questions as well as constructed response questions.

7

Designing Your Assessment

Design is not just what it looks like and feels like. Design is how it works.

Steve Jobs

The Set Up of Your Assessment

Now that you understand the state standards as well as its assessment and have constructed your pacing guide, you can put into practice what you have learned about writing questions. You must design an assessment that will evaluate how well your students have learned the standards. The operative word here is *design*. It is not as simple as going through the pacing guide and writing a question for each standard. This may provide you too few questions or it may cause you to have 10 constructed response questions and only 3 multiple-choice questions. It might even cause you to have all lower-level thinking questions and no higher-level ones. You have to design these assessments so that you have a good mix, bringing you to step 4 in the SCORE Process.

Figure 7.1 Step 4 in the SCORE Process: Design Assessment

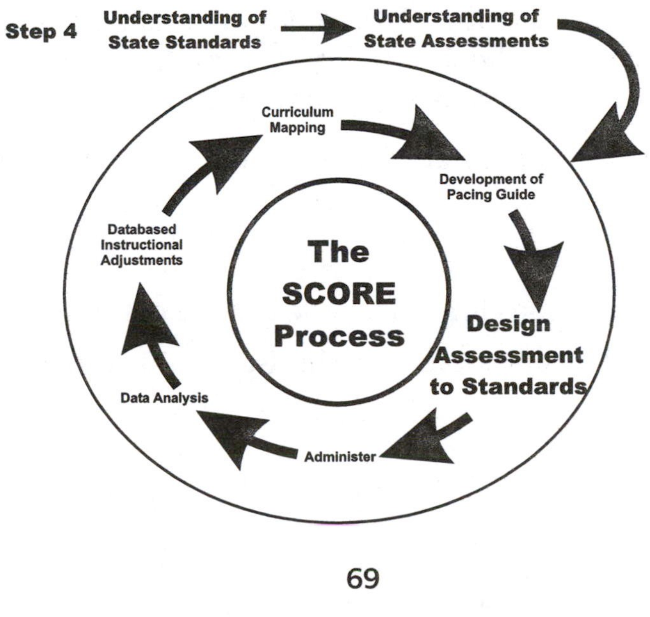

There are five things you want to consider when setting up your short-cycle assessment.

1. Number of questions
2. Number of multiple-choice and constructed response questions
3. Number of higher-level/lower-level questions
4. Spelling and grammar
5. Matching the standard to its level of Bloom's taxonomy

The first consideration is the *number of questions*. Remember that these are *short*-cycle assessments and are not supposed to be the same length as the state assessment. That is why you developed the pacing guide so as to spread these standards out over the course of the school year. Your short-cycle assessment is supposed to be a snapshot of what the state assessment will look like. We typically recommend from 15 to 25 questions on a short-cycle assessment. There are two reasons for the minimum of 15: First, anything less would not provide enough data to determine student progress. Second, you are trying to build up the test-taking endurance of your students. Students need to get used to taking these formatted tests and sitting for an extended period of time. Anything too short will not build this endurance. The other side of the coin is that more than 25 questions would be too long and test the patience of your students. You do not want to burn them out on the short-cycle assessment process especially considering they could be taking four or more assessments over the course of the school year.

Next, consider the number of multiple-choice, constructed response, response grid, and writing prompt questions for the assessment you are writing. The mix of questions should be the same percentage as the state assessment. If you are from a state with only multiple-choice questions, you do not have to concern yourself with this mix because all your questions will be multiple-choice. Many states do have a mix of questions and you want to replicate this on your short-cycle assessment, mirroring the state assessment and the ratio of questions it has. You can use a formula to figure out the breakdown of different questions on the state assessment as it relates to your short-cycle assessment. Here is an example:

35 of 50 questions on the state test are made up of multiple-choice questions

$35 \div 50 = 0.7$

0.7×20 total questions for short-cycle assessment $= 14$

<u>14</u> multiple-choice questions on a short-cycle assessment

10 of 50 questions on the state test are made up of two-point constructed response questions

$10 \div 50 = 0.2$

0.2×20 total questions for short-cycle assessment = 4

<u>4</u> two-point constructed response questions on a short-cycle assessment

5 of 50 questions on the state test are made up of multiple-choice questions

$5 \div 50 = 0.1$

0.1×20 total questions for short-cycle assessment = 2

<u>2</u> four-point constructed response questions on a short-cycle assessment

You can figure out the formula for your own state assessment using the *Questions Conversion Chart* (p.146).

You need to be sure that on a 15-question test, that 10 of the 15 questions are not constructed response questions with only 5 multiple-choice questions. You do not want to overexpose your students to constructed response questions because it can cause burnout or a hesitant student to shut down. Where you put these questions can also be an issue. Some teachers prefer to place all the constructed response questions at the end because they have to be hand-graded and then run all the multiple-choice through a scanning device. You do not want to do this unless your state sets up its assessment in this manner. Putting all of the constructed response questions at the end of the test can try your students' endurance. If the state mixes constructed response questions amongst multiple-choice questions, your assessment should do the same. By mixing them in, students get a break between writing responses to the constructed response questions.

The third consideration when designing your assessment is the *number of higher-level and lower-level questions in the assessment*. We believe that aiming for 50% higher-level questions on a short-cycle assessment is a good target. Although you can never have too many higher-level questions on an assessment, you can have too few. If you are short of higher-level choices because the standards in your pacing guide are of the lower-level variety, you can always write the questions to a higher level. If you determine that your finished short-cycle assessment does not have at least half higher-level questions, you may need to rewrite some questions to make them higher level.

The fourth consideration when designing your assessment questions is *spelling and grammar*. Although spelling errors are not the end of the world you do want the assessment to look as professional as possible and nothing is more unprofessional than an assessment with a lot of mistakes. You need to make sure that, in addition to the questions being correct, the reading passages and any graphics used also are as they should be.

Finally, the most important aspect of your assessment is making sure that your *questions match the standard and the level on the Taxonomy Table.* Remember that it is acceptable to go above the level of the standard, but never below. If you do not write the question to the standard, you will receive inaccurate data when assessing whether or not the student has mastered the standard. The student may have mastered the standard at a lower level but cannot show mastery at the level it was intended and you will not get the information you need to make good instructional decisions.

Use of Reading Passages and Graphics

We recommend using reading passages and graphics in your assessment no matter what subject area you teach. The reason is that most state assessments include a good amount of reading passages and graphics so it is a good idea to get your students used to these. Often times the information a student needs to answer the question is located in the reading passage or the graphic, so if you can help your students become strong at this skill, you will be giving them a big advantage.

Graphics—charts, graphs, illustrations, etc.—also need to be presented to your students on a regular basis. Students need to understand that graphics are just another way to present information and they need to be able to glean as much understanding from them as possible. Guided instruction on how to read graphics, along with practice in both reading and creating graphics, will provide the students with the exposure they need to answer questions on an assessment that uses a lot of graphics.

As for the number of reading passages, given a 15- to 25-question assessment, 2 to 3 reading passages are ample with anywhere from 3 to 5 questions connected to each passage. If there are fewer questions than this per selection, your students may feel it is not worth the effort to read the passage. At the same time, too many questions per passage and you are asking your students to hold onto the information over a long stretch of time. You do not want to have all the questions on the short-cycle assessment connected to reading passages unless that is the way your state assessment sets up its assessment. You will want to have what we term "stand alone" questions that do not require the use of a reading passage to answer. Most state assessments use a combination of the two.

It goes without saying that reading passages should be grade-level appropriate. You do not want to provide extremely easy reading passages on your short-cycle assessments only to have your students come across difficult ones on the state assessment. Examining your state assessment to see the average length of its reading passages will allow you to model this on your own short-cycle assessment.

Social studies assessments should contain maps, as students will probably have to demonstrate their geography skills, and science assessments should include graphs or charts to ready students for these types of questions. Math assessments should contain graphs and data charts to reflect the specific skills required, and reading assessments should include graphic organizers to aid comprehension.

The Answer Key

The answer key may seem inconsequential to some but a mistake on it can cause a lot of problems. Putting the wrong multiple-choice answer can result in a teacher marking a question wrong on an entire set of assessments, resulting in students receiving a lower score and skewing the data. At the same time, an incomplete answer for the constructed response questions can result in a lot of ambiguity and subjectiveness as to the way a teacher grades these items. Consequently, on the answer key for a constructed response question you have to be as clear as possible as to what the student can and cannot have as a correct answer. When there is a question that requires a student opinion, often times teachers want the answer key to read: Answers will vary. There needs to be more guidance than that. A better answer is:

> Student will include opinion and back this up with details and/or examples pertaining to the question. Students answers should not contain any-one else's opinion but theirs.

It is also a good idea to be clear in a multipart question how each point can be attained. For instance, for the question:

> Our country depends on energy usage. What is the energy source we rely the most on? Name three different sources of alternative energy. Compare and contrast the advantages and disadvantages of these three alternative energy sources. Argue which of the three you feel is most important and why.

Your answer key should look something like this:

> 1 pt. — oil
>
> 1 pt. — Answers will vary but may include wind, solar, water, steam; cannot use coal or petroleum
>
> 1 pt. — Answers will vary but should include a legitimate advantage and disadvantage for each of the three energy sources
>
> 1 pt. — Student must choose one of the three and include why they have chosen it using details and examples

Sometimes a way to describe appropriate answers is to describe an answer that would be unacceptable. In the question...

> What was your favorite part of the story and why?

...you would want to include on the answer key

Unacceptable Answer: "Because I liked it."

Sometimes the unacceptable example better tells the teacher about what is acceptable than do a dozen examples of acceptable answers. You also need to keep in mind that you do not have to include every single example a student might think of. This would be next to impossible, especially in a critical thinking, open-ended question. It is most often enough to write

Examples may include … …, etc.

The rule of thumb for the answer key is that someone who did not create the assessment could grade it exactly as the classroom teacher would based solely on the integrity of the answer key. If this is the case, then the answer key is where it needs to be. If you do not think this is possible, there needs to be some revision.

The Answer Booklet

In many cases students are asked to write the answers to their questions in a separate answer booklet or sheet. In some cases this is grade-level oriented. By that we mean that in grades K–4, for instance, the student may be allowed to record their answers on the assessment itself, whereas in grades 5 and up they are required to answer in a separate booklet or sheet. As you know some students will have trouble with this transference. The best way to combat this is to provide them with practice and perhaps even some modeling on how best to structure this. Therefore, we suggest that you provide the students with answer booklet or sheets that mirror the state assessment. We know that many times teachers, schools, and school districts are reluctant to do this because of paper shortages, but it will be worth the sacrifice in the end. The last thing you want is for your students to become confused and miss a question because they do not understand where to write the answer.

The Importance of Revising and Editing

One point we want to make emphatically clear is that this is an ongoing process. Even after all your assessments have been written and you have the process down, you need to continue to revise and revisit your assessments, pacing guides, and classroom instruction. With this in mind, expect your first assessment to be imperfect, but make it as close to perfect as you can. This assessment is supposed to get students ready for the high-stakes assessment by exposing them to a similar test, as well as acting as a diagnostic tool for you to determine student progress. That is why it is important for the assessment to be continuously revised so as to improve its accuracy as a diagnostic tool.

The revising and editing process is more than just a spell check or a crossing of the t's or a dotting of the i's. Revising and editing also means looking at the size and type of the font, making sure pictures are readable (remember that you are going to be making copies and sometimes sharpness of maps or graphs get lost in the process), and that a question is not split over two pages. Check the overall appearance of the assessment to make sure it is how you want it to look.

The Process of Revising and Editing

Once you have taken all the standards from your pacing guide and written 15 to 25 questions, you should conduct a careful revising and editing session. The procedure we suggest is for you to sit down with your short-cycle assessment, a copy of the standards you are covering in their full text form, the Taxonomy Table, and *Revising and Editing Worksheet* (p. 147). We also recommend that you do this at least a day or two after you have developed the questions. It helps to strengthen the objectivity needed to effectively revise and edit a question if you have had some time between the struggle to write the question and the actual revising and editing session.

We like to use a group approach (collaborative grade level or content teachers) to revising and editing an assessment. Typically, the session begins with the standard the question is assessing read out loud. Next, the question is read aloud. The purpose is to be sure the question does indeed measure the skill the Content Standard is laying out. Once you have determined the question is true to the standard, you want to check the verb of the standard and the Taxonomy Table to determine if the standard has been written to the appropriate level of Bloom's taxonomy. Following that you check the format of the question: Are there enough answer choices for the multiple-choice questions? Are the distracters similar? Do the constructed response questions measure a different skill for each part of the questions, and are the number of parts/points clear to the student?

This process should be followed for every question, using the *Revising and Editing Worksheet* (p. 147) to help guide this part of the process. The *Revising and Editing Worksheet* (p. 148) is an second worksheet that uses a different approach. It is included so you can use the worksheet that is most effective for your situation. Once you have checked the entire assessment, move on to the *Assessment Checklist* (p. 149) to be sure you have covered all the major requirements. If you answer "no" to any of the questions on the checklist, you need to revise the assessment.

Finally, after all that is done, complete the *Pacing Guide Confirmation* (p. 150). This ensures you have covered all the standards you intended to cover on the pacing guide for this short-cycle assessment. If you have forgotten any, write a question to address that standard.

Writing Assessment Checklist (p. 151) and *Reading Assessment Checklist* (p. 152) are for the subject areas of writing and reading, and *General Assessment Checklist* (p. 153) is a general checklist for math, science, and social studies. Although they may not apply exactly to your assessment, they will give you an idea of what you should include on your short-cycle assessment.

Revising After You have Given the Assessment

After you have given your assessment you will see the glaring mistakes that were overlooked in the revising and editing process, either because students will point items out or you will notice them yourself in the grading process. There will be all sorts of errors, ranging from misspellings, grammar, awkward sentences, poor copy quality, to questions that just weren't very good. Our advice is not to wait to revise these mistakes. The longer you wait the more you forget about what the problems were. However, we caution you to not change questions to make them easier because it appears a question is too difficult for your students.

The approach we suggest for teachers to take when revising after giving a short-cycle assessment is this: Sit down either by yourself or in a group (if you gave the assessment as part of a team of teachers) and list the issues you discovered when you gave the assessment. Do not touch the actual assessment but write these issues either on a chalkboard, a piece of chart paper, or even a piece of notebook paper. It is important to resist the urge to solve the problems with the questions. You simply want the issues recorded for future reference. After listing the issues go through the data analysis section in Chapter 9, filling out the data analysis worksheet and reflection. Only after doing this should you go back with a clean copy of the assessment and make your changes.

The reason we have teachers do it this way is because following the data analysis they are less likely to change questions that are good but were complex or difficult. The data analysis helps the teachers look at the way a skill was instructed. This prevents a good question from getting jettisoned just because a teacher thought it was "too hard."

Once you have done this you can either tuck this revised assessment away to be typed later or retype it then so it is ready to give the following year. Some teachers like to wait until they have done a few more assessments because they will learn more and will produce a better revision of the first assessment.

The Short of Designing Your Assessment

Here is a review of what we covered in designing your assessment:

- ◆ Number of questions
  - Should be 15 to 25 questions long
- ◆ Number of multiple-choice and constructed response questions (response grids and writing prompts where applicable)
  - Ratio should model the state assessment
- ◆ Number of higher-level/lower-level questions

- • Need at least half or more to be higher level
- ◆ Spelling and grammar
  - • Need to check it as you don't want a student to not understand the question as a result of misspellings or confusing sentence structure
- ◆ Matching the question to the standard and its level of Bloom's taxonomy
  - • Most important aspect to be sure students are actually demonstrating mastery of the standard at or above the level of the standard

You also need to type the assessment using the same size and style font as the state assessment. Do as much as you can to model the state assessment including the directions and the rubrics so that students are as accustomed to the state style as possible.

Eventually you will use this assessment-designing method to write however many short-cycle assessments you indicated at the beginning of this process. After you have all your assessments in place you want to revise the assessments based on what you have learned so as to make your first attempts stronger. This is your decision, but the more comfortable you become writing questions the more likely you will want to improve the ones you wrote when you did not have that confidence or level of expertise.

The revising and editing of the assessment is almost as important as the initial writing of it. You want an assessment that looks professional and exposes students to what the high-stakes test looks like. Make sure to give it a thorough revising and editing, correcting mistakes and giving the assessment a clean polish.

8

Standardization of Administration

Human beings, by changing the inner attitudes of their minds, can change the outer aspects of their lives.

William Jones

Attitude of the Teachers

One of the most important factors in the success of the SCORE Process lies within the attitude of the teachers who administer it. When implementing this process in a school, nothing spells trouble more quickly than teachers who do not take the assessments and administration of them seriously. A teacher's attitude can be contagious. Think about the teachers who had the most influence on you as a student. Those teachers with the passionate attitude toward their subject were always the ones whose class was more meaningful as well as interesting. This attitude carries over to the students and produces high-quality learning.

We once worked with teachers on analyzing data from a short-cycle assessment that had been given shortly after the high-stakes state test. The one recurring statement we kept hearing from the teachers was that this particular short-cycle assessment was too close to the actual test and the students were so burned out they didn't even want to try. This was a perfect opportunity to stress the importance of attitude so we asked the teachers how they had administered this particular assessment. We said to the teachers, "When you passed out this assessment did you say to the students, "Okay, class, we have one more assessment to take. I know that you are burned out from taking assessments and the truth is so am I.", or did you say, "Okay class, we have one more assessment to take. Now I know that you are so ready to take this test and have had a lot of practice. You can nail this test and succeed just as well as you have on the others." As we looked around the room we could see teachers looking at one another sheepishly as they began to realize that they had presented the assessment in the former way rather than the latter. They had not stopped to consider that they could make such a difference in their students' attitudes toward the assessment. Once they approached the assessment in the latter way, they were surprised at the sense of positive energy that was emulating throughout the room and what a difference it made in the results.

The same goes for the short-cycle assessments. We're not saying you have to be passionate about giving the exams, but when a teacher goes in with the attitude of "I really do not want to give this test; it is only going to take away from valuable class time," students will easily sense this and carry this attitude into their performance on the assessment. That is why it is important to be consistent in your administration of the short-cycle assessment. This brings us to step 5 of the SCORE Process: Administer (Figure 8.1)

Figure 8.1 Step 5 of the SCORE Process: Administer

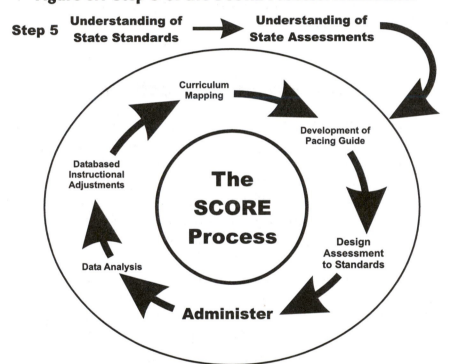

It is important that you be upfront with your students about the rationale for taking these short-cycle assessments. Explain to them how they will be used to guide instruction—you will be able to concentrate your teaching on what the students don't know rather than waste their time on what they already do know. If students understand this and you stress the importance of it, they will (hopefully) try their best and show you where they are in regard to an understanding of the Content Standards. If you explain that if they have a poor showing on the short-cycle assessment, the material may need to be covered again and they will have to relearn something they already have learned, the students are more likely to take it seriously. Keep in mind that students will only take the assessment as seriously as you do.

To Review or Not to Review?

One aspect that might be different than when students are getting ready for a regular classroom test is that with your short-cycle assessments you should not do any in-class review of what you have covered and what will be on the assessment. The rationale for this is that the assessment is designed to collect information to see if your students have learned the Content Standards your pacing guide says they should have learned. In other words, do your students have enduring understanding of the skills and have they actually learned what was taught? If you review with them right before the short-cycle assessment or provide them with a review guide, students won't necessarily be showing you what they have mastered. Instead, they just may be recalling the information from the review you provided.

This part of the short-cycle assessment process is not very comfortable for some people. Many of us have considered review to be an important part of good instructional practice. As teachers, we often feel compelled to give our students whatever edge we can provide them because we believe these assessments are a reflection of our ability to teach. This is one point in the process where we are asking teachers to step out of the box and look at assessments as a way to get information, not as a way to give a student a grade. It is imperative to know how a student is going to perform on the high-stakes test. That means the good, the bad, and the ugly.

It may help to think of this part of the process in the following way: Suppose you were taking your car in for its final checkup just before the warranty expires. Would you want your mechanic to temporarily fix the things that are wrong with your car so that a couple of months later it breaks down and you are stuck with a high repair bill? Of course not. You want to know what is wrong with your car before the warranty runs out so that things can be fixed without any cost to you. The same analogy goes for your students. You need to fix the things that are wrong with your students with regard to their learning prior to the state assessment. Reviewing before the assessment may fix things for the short-term, but later, when the warranty runs out, those same students may be forced to pay dearly if the repairs are not made on a long-term basis for enduring understanding.

Remember the goal is not for all students to pass with high grades. The goal is to see what students truly understand and expose any gaps there might be. You want all the warts and blemishes to appear on this short-cycle assessment rather than on the state test. If students perform poorly on these short-cycle assessments, there is something you can do about it, which is how the process is designed. If they perform poorly on the high-stakes test, there is nothing that can be done to change it.

The Assessment Administration Schedule

If you are administering your short-cycle assessments as common assessments throughout an entire grade level or school it is best that the testing schedule model what the high-stakes assessment will look like. For instance, your state may give one assessment a day over the course of a week. If this is the case in your state, your schedule should copy this—taking the short-cycle math on Tuesday, reading on Wednesday, and science on Thursday. That way students are used to which subjects will be tested when and can prepare for them accordingly.

Likewise your testing schedule may have multiple tests administered on a single day. If this is the case, you too would want to take all your short-cycle assessments in a single day. This gets students used to the pacing of the test-taking and builds up their test-taking endurance.

Some teachers believe those subjects that are later in the week have an advantage because students are used to the process and format. Other teachers think it is a disadvantage because students have become burned out of test taking by that time and do not give their best effort. If you have prepared students correctly using the SCORE Process, neither should be a problem.

The time of day the assessments are given is also something to consider. Some assessments are given in the morning with the afternoon spent in regular classes, whereas others are flipped the opposite way. Because many times schools are the ones to determine when the state assessment will be administered, check with your school testing coordinator and model this.

You will want to provide a time limit for your short-cycle assessment because most of the high-stakes tests have them. Because the short-cycle assessments are shorter than the state test, you will have to adjust the time allowed to take the assessment. You must give students enough time to take the assessment, yet impose enough of a time limit that students begin to pace themselves, learning how to adjust their test-taking skills to move past difficult questions that may cause them to get stuck. If possible, you should also provide scheduled breaks so students get used to having to stop and restart the assessment.

Administration Should Be the Same

Your administration of the short-cycle assessment should put the students in a dry run of the high-stakes test. You should provide an atmosphere that is very similar to the state test, whether it be the set up of the room, the rules in the classroom during the assessment, the seriousness you place on the situation, or even the bathroom policy and placement of the desks and Kleenex. During many state assessments, protocol requires you to hang a sign outside your classroom to indicate that people need to be quiet and respect those taking the tests. You should use such signs for your short-cycle assessments to create the correct environment. *Do Not Disturb* (p. 154) is a sample sign that can be copied.

Another thing to consider is the seating of your students. You will need to emulate whatever seating arrangement you use for your state test. If your students take the state test in a large group setting, that is what you should provide them with on the short-cycle assessments. If someone other than yourself will administer the state assessment, then that person(s) should administer the short-cycle assessments. If you are a teacher who has no assigned seating in your classroom, then you should assign seats for the short-cycle assessments if that is what is done for the high-stakes test. This will help the students adjust to having a seat assigned to them during the state test. Likewise, it is important to have your students work alone and quietly during this time. In this day of cooperative learning, students need to learn the difference between a group work environment and a testing environment. Imagine the teacher who encourages their students to sit wherever they choose and ask their peers for help whenever they need it. Then comes a time, once a year, when suddenly they are not allowed to move from the seat they have been assigned to nor are they allowed to ask for help. You can certainly understand how this could invoke panic in even the most confident student. Again, the idea is to practice everything about the high-stakes test—from the material taught to the testing environment. We want the students to feel comfortable and the best way to accomplish this is to prepare them in every way.

One way to set up this testing atmosphere is to provide verbal directions much like many of the state assessments do. Figure 8.2 is a page from the testing directions provided by NECAP (New England Commission Assessment Program) whose assessments are used in New Hampshire, Rhode Island, and Vermont.

Figure 8.2 Testing Directions

Mathematics — Session 1

Estimated Time: 45 Minutes

Materials needed: Student Test Booklets, Student Answer Booklets, Mathematics Reference Sheets, scratch paper, and #2 pencils.

NOTE: Use of rulers, protractors, calculators, NECAP Multiplication Tables, and NECAP Hundreds Charts is *not* permitted during Session 1 of the mathematics test.

1. Return the Student Test Booklets and Student Answer Booklets to students. Each student must have his or her original test materials. Distribute a Mathematics Reference Sheet to each student and instruct them to write their names on it. Distribute scratch paper to all students and instruct them to write their names on it. Distribute #2 pencils to students who need them.

2. Say to the students:

    You are now going to start Session 1 of the mathematics test. Please turn to page 26 in your Student Test Booklet. (Pause.) In this session, you will answer twenty-one questions. Some of the questions may be hard for you to answer, but it is important that you do your best. If you are not sure of the answer to a question, you should make your best guess. Do not mark your answers in the Student Test Booklet. Instead, mark your answers for this session on pages 12, 13, & 14 of your Student Answer Booklet. Choose the best answer for each multiple-choice question and plan your written answers so they fit only in the answer spaces in your Student Answer Booklet.

    You may use your scratch paper to plan your answers and make notes, but only what you write in the answer spaces in your Student Answer Booklet will be scored. Some questions have more than one part. Try to answer all of the parts. If you are asked to explain or show how you know, be sure to copy all of your work from the scratch paper into your Student Answer Booklet. Does anyone have any questions? (Answer any questions the students have about the directions.)

3. Say to the students:

    Open your Student Answer Booklet to page 12. The top of the page is labeled "Mathematics – Session 1." It will probably take you about 45 minutes to answer the questions in this session of the test, but you can have more time if you want it.

    Please stop when you come to the stop sign at the end of this session. You may review your answers to the questions in this session of the test, but you may not go forward or go back to work on any other sessions.

    If you get stuck on a word, I can read the word to you. I cannot read numbers, mathematics symbols, or a whole question to you. If you want help reading a word, raise your hand. (Pronounce the word to students who asked for assistance. Do not define the word or help the students in any other way.) Are there any questions? (Answer any questions the students have about the directions.) When you finish, insert your Student Answer Booklet, Mathematics Reference Sheet, and scratch paper into your Student Test Booklet. Please sit quietly and read until everyone is finished. You may begin.

These directions provide a script for teachers to follow when giving the assessments. Using a similar script for your own short-cycle assessments will put students in the situation of testing and provide them with the right mindset. *Directions to Read to Students* (p. 155) is a general script for verbal directions, but feel free to create your own based upon your own state test using the *Assessment Directions Sheet* (p. 156).

Providing or allowing the same materials or resources for your short-cycle assessment as is allowed for the state test is also a good idea. Many states give teachers a checklist of appropriate materials. Whether you have a checklist or not, you should provide and require the same materials and resources for your students on the short-cycle assessments that are required for the state test.

Many times the resources and materials that are provided during the state test are not the same resources and materials that the teachers have access to on a daily basis in their classrooms. One example of this is calculators in math in the primary grades, or beginner's dictionaries in language arts in the primary grades. Someone in your school district should be responsible for taking an inventory of the materials required for the state test and then make sure that each classroom is provided with the same materials. If you find anything in your standards that require materials or resources you do not have, you need to make this clear to the district personnel responsible for the curriculum.

Speaking of calculators, a point has to be made for the ethical consideration of the use of materials during a testing situation. Whenever you are not sure about the use of materials, ask yourself an important question: Is this practice going to hinder student success on the state test? If the answer is "yes" or even "maybe," then perhaps the practice is not what is best for your students. Sometimes we teachers have to be willing to make changes even in our basic philosophies so as to better serve our students. Certainly, the answer to this predicament is probably a compromise—sometimes using the materials, and sometimes not. Whatever you decide, keep in mind that you do not want to place your students at a disadvantage on the high-stakes test just because you believe you need to take a philosophical stand.

Another thing to consider is the amount and type of accommodations given on the state test. States allow certain accommodations because of handicaps, learning disabilities, and other reasons. Your testing environment should model the accommodations the state test would allow. You do not want to provide accommodations for students on the short-cycle assessments and then have them taken away on the high-stakes test. You want students to be familiar and comfortable with the accommodations provided for them.

The Short of Standardization of Administration

The three most important aspects of administering your short-cycle assessments are attitude, attitude, and attitude. Oh, and don't forgot, attitude is pretty important too. The attitude you carry in the classroom about the testing will reflect in your students and whether they care about them. One of the most important things you can do for your students is to explain to them exactly why they are taking these short-cycle assessments and the benefits for them.

Another important aspect is to think of the short-cycle assessments as a dress rehearsal for the high-stakes state test. That means that everyone is in costume and makeup, all the sets are complete, and you run it through just like you would if it were opening night. Making your short-cycle assessment administration as much like the high-stakes test as possible insures that your students won't be caught unaware or off-guard.

9

Looking at the Data

Statistician: a (person) who believes figures don't lie, but admits that under analysis some of them won't stand up either.

Evan Esar

The Problem with Data

As teachers we can be inundated with data any time we choose. There are folders full of test scores, teacher evaluations, and numbers concerning our students that have valuable information. The only problem is you have to know how to look for the useful information amongst all of the other things in those cumulative folders that are not so useful. How often as teachers are we intentionally taught how to use the information in these folders? Looking at these folders can be like looking at something written in a foreign language with all the numbers, acronyms, and different colored papers. This information is many times gathered by people we do not interact with or cannot discuss the importance of, such as prior teachers, school psychologists, or the state department of education.

We as teachers gather data all the time but it is usually after the fact. We find out how students are doing on our lessons using a test at the end of a unit when it may be too late to do anything if students do not "get it." Sure we give our students homework and worksheets to check their progress along the way, but rarely as teachers do we gather really meaningful data that we can immediately put into use to help make sure students are learning what it is we have intended.

The trick to really using data is being able to find data that we can understand and can figure out how to use in the classroom. Here are some tips to getting and using data that can be very helpful to teachers.

- ◆ What You Need to Know
  - • Keep it simple.
  - • Know that you are not alone, others are struggling with this as well.
  - • Student achievement and student ability should match one another.

- There is more than one way to measure student success.

♦ What You Don't Want to Do
  - Go over every single thing in each of your student's files.
  - Over analyze (stick to data that matters).
  - Set too many goals.
  - Set unattainable or unmeasurable goals.

♦ What to Look For
  - Data that is going to directly affect instruction for increased student achievement.
  - Results that do not make sense.
  - Strengths and improvements to be made as a teacher.
  - Data that will help you learn from others and promote collaboration.

Keeping these tips in mind when going through your short-cycle assessments and analyzing the data you get from them will help you to maximize the relevant information.

Data From the Short-Cycle Assessments

Short-cycle assessments are an excellent data gathering source that will give you information that is

♦ Instant

♦ Simple

♦ Usable

This data is *instant* because you get it immediately by using the short-cycle assessments. The assessments do not have to be sent away or deciphered by a nameless, faceless person. The results are there as soon as you grade and analyze them. The data you get from the short-cycle assessments is very *simple*. In some cases the student either masters the skill or does not. There is no interpretation of numbers or trying to figure out a complex formula. You get the score, compare it to others, analyze the reasons for any deviations, and determine what actions need to take place in the classroom to help with these. *Usable* is a very important aspect of the data. As mentioned before, we get a lot of information on our students but how much of it are we actually able to use? The data from the short-cycle assessments will show you adjustments that need to be made in your classroom and can be done very quickly.

That brings us to step 6 in the SCORE Process: Data Analysis (Figure 9.1).

Figure 9.1 Step 6 in the SCORE Process: Data Analysis

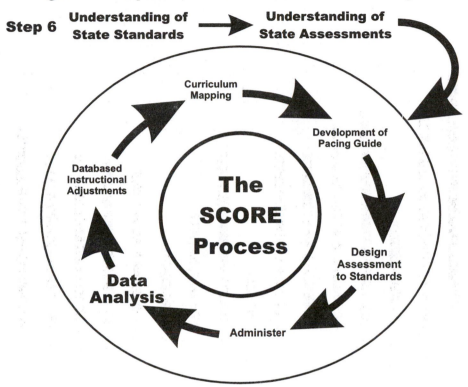

This chapter highlights the various reports that can be produced from your short-cycle assessments as well as how to translate them to the classroom so as to better help your students learn.

Class Profile Graph

The class profile graph, like its namesake, profiles every student in the class that took the assessment and how they scored overall. By gathering this information you can determine whether a majority of your students are "getting it" and if not, which ones specifically are not. This graph lists every student in the class on the Y axis and his or her percentage score on the X axis. Using a bar graph you chart how the individual student performed on the short-cycle assessment. Figure 9.2 is an example of a class profile graph.

Figure 9.2 Class Profile Graph

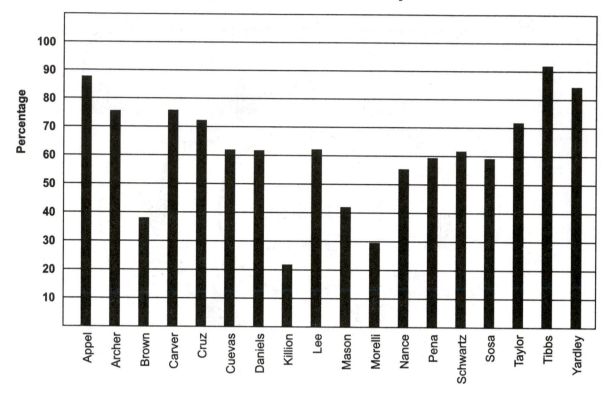

By doing this you can pinpoint which students need intervention. This graph also lets you make sure that student achievement and student ability match one another. Students should not have more than a standard deviation between their classroom grade and their short-cycle assessment score. In other words, if a student is receiving a B in your social studies class, they should not score any lower than a C on the social studies short-cycle assessment. If they do score lower, then their classroom achievement is not matching the ability that the short-cycle assessment should measure. Similarly, if a student is getting a D in your math class, a red flag should go up if they receive a B on the math short-cycle assessment. Somehow their ability is not coming out in their achievement in the class.

The bottommost line is the lower curve line and represents those students falling below what is statistically considered the average for the class. These students will usually be your immediate concern as they are the ones that need more intervention than others. Also be aware of the converse side of things: the topmost line, the upper curve line, represents those students who are performing well-above the rest of the class. Many times the upper curve line will be set at 100% depending on the average score of the class. If you have a student who is above that upper line you may need to differentiate your lessons to challenge that student. Some differentiated lessons may include acceleration activities, tiered lessons, and/or alternative assessments.

Those students who are above or below the curve lines may not be a surprise to you. If a student who is below the lower curve line typically struggles or performs poorly in your class, he or she is probably already receiving intervention strategies. The same goes for a student who continually is at the top of the class and is above the upper curve line. With the class profile graph you need to look for patterns that make sense. Using the standard deviation theory you need to make sure that student achievement and ability match. It is when these do not match or make sense that you look for immediate information for ways to help students. For example, you may have a student who scores an 85% on the short-cycle assessment but is failing the class. Using this data you analyze, much like a detective would, to find answers to this quandary. The student is showing ability so maybe:

- He does not do his homework regularly which pulls his grades down.

- His attendance or behavior causes a lower grade.

- He may be embarrassed socially to do well in class so he underachieves.

- Perhaps a poor home life prevents him from reaching his potential.

- He might have even gotten lucky. We once heard a story about a student who was a big AC/DC music fan and answered his short-cycle assessment with these initials, scoring quite well by chance.

Like any good detective, you will need to investigate the reason behind this difference. That is what analysis involves.

Another important aspect when analyzing data is to look for trends. Never assume that something a student does once is indicative of future performance. If a student performs poorly in comparison to their achievement, and this is something new, several factors could be involved.

- The student may suffer from test anxiety.

- The student may have bubbled in the wrong number once, throwing the sequence off.

- The student may be a poor writer and performed poorly on the constructed response questions, pulling the results down.

- The student may be a hard worker who achieves high grades because of his hard work, and not his ability.

- The student may not have been feeling well the day of the assessment or have forgotten to have breakfast and was feeling lightheaded.

These are all possible roads of investigation to pursue while tracking down the reason for an unexpected poor performance on a short-cycle assessment. The class profile graph enables you to pinpoint any anomalies in the performance of an individual student. *Class Profile Graph* (p. 157) provides directions and a template for you to create your own class profile graph.

Classroom Item Analysis Graph

The classroom item analysis graph charts the questions themselves, with the overall average of how the class performed on each question. The Y axis represents each question identified by number, standard, and even format if you choose. The X axis represents the score of percent mastered. Because this is a mastery graph, it is important to remember that on a 1-point multiple-choice question the student will need to get the question correct to earn mastery. At the same time, on a multipoint constructed response question the student will need to score at least 75% or 3 of 4 on a 4-point question or 3 of 3 on a 3-point question. Scoring a 2 of 4 on a 4-point question would only be a 50%, far from mastery.

Figure 9.3 is an example of a classroom item analysis graph.

Figure 9.3 Item Analysis Graph

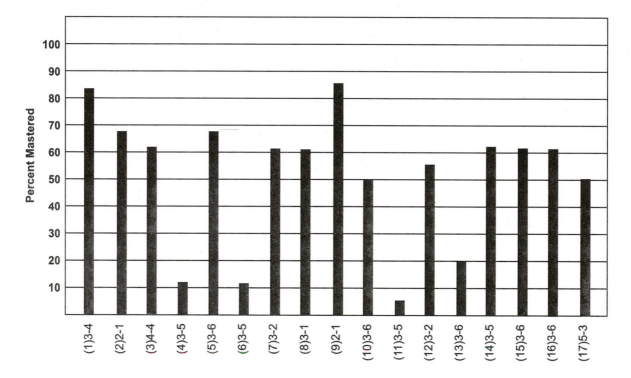

To analyze the data on this particular report you would look for the low-scoring questions and try to discern a pattern. For instance, you may notice on this particular graph that questions 4, 6, and 11 are all from standard 3–5. That means the class overall did not do well on this standard, which indicates it was not taught at a mastery level and probably needs to be retaught. Here are some other patterns we typically will see on the short-cycle assessment along with some instructional implications of how they can be improved for next time:

◆ *Pattern:* Most of the lower-scoring questions are constructed response questions where students have to write their responses.

  • *Instructional implication:* Students need more exposure to multipart questions and writing.

◆ *Pattern:* Most of the lower-scoring questions are higher-level standards.

  • *Instructional implication:* Students need more exposure to higher-level questions in the classroom.

◆ *Pattern:* Most of the higher-scoring questions are lower-level, multiple-choice.

  • *Instructional implication:* Keep exposing your students to these because they are the building blocks for the higher-level questions.

◆ *Pattern:* Lower-scoring questions are coming from the same standard category (i.e., math–probability).

  • *Instructional implication:* This may be a standard that as a teacher is not your strength. We all have strengths and weaknesses as teachers. The key is figuring out a way around your weakness through professional development or collaboration.

◆ *Pattern:* Higher-scoring questions are coming from the same standard category (i.e., math–patterns).

  • *Instructional implication:* This may be a standard that is taught often in whatever textbook/materials you are provided. You may need to adjust the amount of time you spend on this standard, as it may be taking time away from a standard with which your students have more difficulty.

◆ *Pattern:* Students start out strong with higher mastery at the beginning questions, but sort of fade toward the last few questions.

  • *Instructional implication:* Students need to work on one of two things or maybe both: (a) endurance in sitting and taking a test, giving the same effort at the end of the test as the beginning, and/or (b) pacing in taking the test—they may have run out of time and left a few of the questions at the end blank.

Sometimes you won't see an overall pattern in the data, but just isolated questions on which students do poorly. There could be many reasons for this.

◆ The standard wasn't taught either because of lack of time or unforeseen circumstances, such as weather days or too many assemblies.

♦ The standard wasn't taught at the level it needed to be taught because students took longer to grasp it at a lower level.

♦ The answer key was incorrect.

♦ The question wasn't very clear and students misunderstood it or a typographical error caused them to mistake another answer.

If the problem is one of the first two, it becomes an adjustment in the classroom to be sure the students learn all the standards covered at the level at which they are intended. If it is one of the latter two, there may need to be revisions to the assessment itself.

Many times the classroom item analysis graph will indicate where there are questions that need to be revised on your short-cycle assessment because they are not clear or have mistakes. You should not revise a question to make it easier because a majority of the students missed it unless it was too far above grade level. If you feel the urge to do this, remember to ask yourself if the question was truly fair. If you decide it was, then examine how the standard was taught. Many times teachers want to change the question rather than instruction.

Classroom Item Analysis Graph (p. 160) provides directions and a template so you can create your own classroom item analysis graph.

Non-Mastery Report

The non-mastery report is a combination of the class profile graph and classroom item analysis graph. To develop a non-mastery report all you have to do is list each question and which students did not master that particular question. A non-mastery report might look like this:

Question 1, Standard: 5–8

Define and identify types of irony, including verbal, situational, and dramatic, used in literary texts.

Baird, J

Barrow, L

Greenlee, C

Harvey, D

Oliver, J

Sahin, B

Question 2, Standard: 2–3

Infer the literal and figurative meaning of words and phrases and discuss the function of figurative language, including metaphors, similes, idioms, and puns.

Barrow, L

Boyer, K

Fu, W

Harvey, D

Sahin, B

Question 3, Standard: 2–3

Infer the literal and figurative meaning of words and phrases and discuss the function of figurative language, including metaphors, similes, idioms and puns.

Barrow, L

Browning, J

Harvey, D

Heveron, A

Kohnen, A

Sahin, B

The value of such a report is that it enables you to figure out flexible grouping in the classroom for differentiated instruction. If you see that six students missed question #1 and the standard needs to be retaught, you can group those students together and do so without having to include those students who mastered that particular standard. At the same time, a question under which most of the class appears would indicate the need to reteach that standard to the entire class.

The non-mastery report gives you a good idea where you need to differentiate without creating permanent groups. We need to have flexible grouping in the classroom not only to move students who are at different levels, but to place emphasis on different areas according to what the students need. Just because someone is an A student it does not mean that student mastered everything; conversely, because someone is failing your class it does not mean they are not getting some things. *Non-Mastery Report* (p. 95) gives directions and provides a template so you can create your own non-mastery report.

Data Analysis

Now that you have this data you have to break it down to make it usable. Giving the short-cycle assessments is only the beginning. With the assessments graded and the graphs in hand, you have to figure out how you can use them to make your classroom an even more successful environment. As stated before, you have to begin to look for trends or patterns in the data and what that might mean for individual students as well as the class as a whole. You will begin to understand where each student is and where they need to go if you are preparing them for mastering the Content Standards.

We ask teachers to look at their five most successful questions and their five least successful questions and what these might mean. There is no handy formula as to what is a successful question and what is not. Some teachers consider only questions on which the students score 75% or higher as successful, whereas other teachers simply eyeball the item analysis graph and choose the top five questions. The choice is yours. Whatever criteria you use, the questions you will want to ask yourself remain the same. Are the least successful questions all the constructed response, higher-level questions from a particular standard? What are the patterns and what do these patterns indicate about adjustments that need to be made in the classroom? What about the most successful questions as far as similarities? Are they the lower-level multiple-choice questions? What does that mean?

Data analysis can be done with a group of teachers or individually. Group analysis is preferable because it gives you many perspectives and opinions about the various patterns. You also will receive some validation for patterns you see with your students that are duplicated by the experiences of other teachers and their students. Do not underestimate the importance of an individual data analysis. It is imperative that you to reflect on your class performance and what that may mean for your own future instruction. You might have different adjustments to make than other teachers as a result of your expertise in certain standards and weaknesses in others. We recommend that you first complete the individual data reflection found in *Individual Assessment Reflection* (p. 164) and bring the results to the group analysis. One thing that is very valuable at these sessions is the opportunity to collaborate. Through collaboration you might discover ways to teach something you had not considered before or share a lesson plan that you have found to work well with students. After each short-cycle assessment you might ask different questions than previously; in that case, you can use the *Group Data Analysis #1* (p. 165), *Group Data Analysis #2* (p. 166), *Group Data Analysis #3* (p. 167), and *Group Data Analysis #4* (p. 168) templates. These templates will walk you step-by-step through what questions to ask and where to look for the answers to those questions.

The Short of Looking at the Data

The short-cycle assessments provide you with data that is:

- Instant

- Simple

- Usable

You need to look at the assessment from the viewpoints of the individual student and the class as a whole to discover patterns or trends for improvement. Where are individual students and the class as a whole deficient and, more importantly, how can you make adjustments in the classroom to see these deficiencies improve? What goals will you set for yourself for the next time and how will you measure these? Don't forget to celebrate success. You don't want to just look for places where students failed. Find successes and share them with the class, acknowledging the good job they did. Your data can speak volumes but if you don't do anything about it, it really doesn't say anything.

10

Making Adjustments in the Classroom

The great aim of education is not knowledge but action.

Herbert Spencer

Using Data to Make Meaningful Changes

The question becomes, once you discover what needs to be improved, how do you do it? That brings us to step 7 of the SCORE Process: Data-Based Instructional Adjustments (Figure 10.1).

**Figure 10.1 Step 7 of the SCORE Process:
Data-Based Instructional Adjustments**

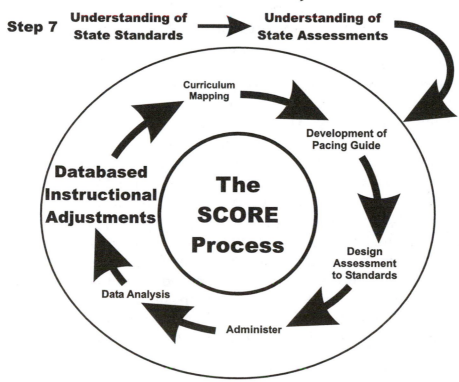

Making changes in the way we teach, even small ones can be uncomfortable. We are used to doing things a certain way and when we feel forced to change, we are sometimes resistant, just like certain students who are resistant when they do not understand. Put yourself in your students' place. When you were taught something new, where did your most meaningful learning occur? Was it where you were the most comfortable and things came easy, or was it where there was a little risk and some discomfort? We call this the zones of learning (Figure 10.2)

Figure 10.2 Zones of Learning

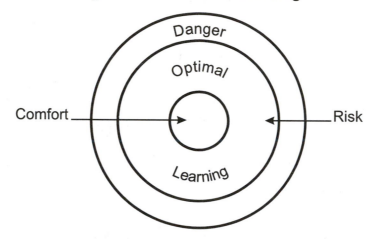

The center of the circle is the comfort zone. In this zone we are typically relaxed, body language open. We feel pretty sure that nobody is going to ask us to perform, or if they do ask, it is to do something we easily know. Sometimes in this zone we are only half listening. The area of the circle surrounding the comfort zone is the risk zone, the place where challenging goals are provided to the learner and some accountability is expected. You are paying close attention. This is the zone in which optimal learning takes place. The final zone, the danger zone, is where the stress level is just too high. As learners we feel threatened when we are in this zone. Our body language is closed and we are usually not listening or trying at this point. When we are pushed into this zone, we either flee or fight. The *How Did You Learn What Was Taught?* (p. 169) activity will help you explore this idea further.

The implications for you as a teacher are that you have to be careful not to do too much that is different. Otherwise you chance crossing over to the danger zone where learners simply shut down because the subject matter is too foreign. Similarly with your own adjustments in the classroom, you do not want to do too much at once. Choose one or two improvements you wish to make in the classroom based on the short-cycle assessment data. It is important that you set these improvements as your goals for the grading period. There needs to be certain stipulations with these goals, otherwise your pursuit of them can be frustrating because they are either unrealistic or unmeasurable. We recommend an action plan called SMART Goals.

Setting SMART Goals

One way to organize your teaching goals is to use the SMART goal system, which many people in the business world use:

S   **strategic**

     will give the greatest "bang for the buck"

M   **measurable**

     includes a method for assessing whether or not the goal is reached

A   **attainable**

     can be done by you and your fellow teachers

R   **results oriented**

     is focused on changing performance within the classroom

T   **time-bound**

     has a timeframe in which the progress will be measured

By using the SMART system, you can keep your goals manageable. You have figured out the *strategic* part by completing the analysis of your short-cycle assessments and determining what the instructional implications are. *Measurable* is an important factor. You should not set a goal such as "students will improve their attitude" for a couple of reasons. First, you personally have no way to control that aspect. Second, there is no way to measure improvement in the attitude of the students. The goal you set needs to be one that can be controlled and measured. The goal must be *attainable* so be sure to reach for goals that are realistic. The goal must be *results oriented* or one in which you have an end result in mind. Finally, the goal must be *time-bound*. You set the goal and with it a deadline for when you want to achieve that goal. Because the short-cycle assessments are administered every grading period, you can set that time period for your improvement. Figure 10.3 is an example of a SMART goals guide by a math teacher.

Figure 10.3 SMART Goals Guide

SMART Goals			
SMART Goal	**Indicators**	**Measurement**	**Targets**
Specific and strategic, measurable, attainable, results-oriented, time bound	Standards and objectives for gaps in performance (what is not there, not measured, or not acceptable...)	Tools you will use to determine improvement from where your school is now to whether they are improving	The attainable performance level that you would like to see by June, 2008
Smart Goal	*Indicators*	*Measurement Method*	*Target for Measurement*
85% of the students taking assessment 3 in March will demonstrate mastery on the measurement indicator (students can convert temperatures from metric to US units) in 100% of the application and analysis questions.	Short-cycle Assessment 3 Data: ♦ 25% of the students demonstrated mastery level of question # 8 ♦ 55% of the students demonstrated mastery level of question # 11 ♦ 47% of the students demonstrated mastery level of question # 17	Assessment 3 student performances for questions 8, 11, and 17 Classroom performance on worksheets 23 and 24 from the Math Workbook	Students answer the short answer questions (8) with 100% accuracy for 100% of the students. Students answer the multiple-choice questions with 85% accuracy. Students practicing the conversions will complete both worksheets and perform an experiment where they will demonstrate a measurement and conversion that will be observed and recorded by the teacher.

You'll notice in this example (Figure 10.3) that there are very specific *strategic* goals: 85% of students will demonstrate mastery on the measurement standard. The measurement method for the goals is included, using the short-cycle assessment and a worksheet, demonstrating that the goal is *measurable*. The goal is realistic which makes it *attainable*. There is an end goal in mind, the 85% mastery, showing that it is *results oriented*. And there is a deadline of June 2008, showing it to be *time-bound*. *SMART Goals* (p. 170), which is a blank guide will help you create your own action plan. You may want to share your plan with your students so they are aware of what they are striving for as a class. You can even offer incentives to motivate them to achieve the class goal.

How to Make Adjustments

You have figured out the improvements you want to make and have set SMART goals. The next step is determining how to make the adjustments. This section will act as a troubleshooting guide. We will take an issue and make a suggestion of how to make the adjustment. Keep in mind that this chapter provides you with some of the basic concepts of methods such as differentiated instruction, compacting the curriculum, and others, but there are whole series of books on these teaching strategies. If you want to learn more about one or more of these strategies, you should consult books that cover the strategies in more depth.

Issue: Students really struggled with the constructed response questions.

Possible adjustments in the classroom: Introduce more writing in the classroom including a question of the day where the students have to explain in writing how they got their answer.

Some teachers think that writing is strictly confined to the reading or language arts classroom. Writing is a skill that should be stressed across the curriculum—whether it be math, social studies, science, gym, or music class. Students cannot get too much writing. They need to be exposed to writing in different subject areas and in different scenarios so they get to practice. A good way to get students writing and expose them to answering multipart questions they might encounter on the high-stakes test is to have a question of the day.

This is quite simple. You write the question on the chalkboard or post it somewhere in the classroom. You could choose to devote a specific period of class time for students to answer this question, or have them work on it when they finish the work you have set out for the day. You could even assign it as homework. However you choose to present this there has to be a place for feedback to the students so they begin to improve their writing and recognize strategies and techniques for improvement. Here is an example of a question of the day for a math class:

Take the first 10 minutes of class to answer the following question of the day:

In the equation $y - 2x = 3$, where y depends on x, find the value of y when $x = 2.5$. Be sure to explain how you got your answer.

If possible phrase the question so that it seems less academic and asks the opinion of the student. That way it does not seem like an assignment but more like a guided journal. An example of this is shown in this question from a social studies class:

Question of the day to be answered by the end of the class:

Which of the freedoms granted by the First Amendment do you feel is the most important and why? How do you think this country would be different if that freedom was taken away?

The question of the day can be tied into what you are working on in class or can be something completely independent of what you are studying. You can evaluate it for a grade or use it as a tool to sharpen your students' ability to write constructed responses. You could also use it to have the students themselves practice how to grade constructed response questions by trading and grading.

If the question of the day becomes a part of the class culture, students will expect it. They will also become more comfortable with it, sort of like practicing a sport or taking music lessons. They will become more comfortable and improve their writing skills the more they are asked to write. At the same time, being given lessons without any feedback or practicing a sport incorrectly can lead to a poor end result. Your job as the teacher is to provide continual encouragement and feedback for how the individual student can improve. Don't leave writing just to the language arts teacher. Writing is a form of communication that needs to be mastered in all subject areas.

Issue: You have a great disparity between your top students and your bottom students on your class profile graph.

Possible adjustment in the classroom: Differentiated instruction.

With regard to this issue, the question becomes what must a teacher do and where must a teacher start to accommodate the many different types of learners found in all classrooms? The answer can be found in differentiated instruction. Differentiated instruction is a detailed best-practice model, one about which many books have been written. Our purpose here is to provide you with the "short" of differentiated instruction. With that is mind, consider the following descriptors.

- ♦ What differentiated instruction is
  - Proactive
  - Qualitative instead of quantitative
  - Rooted in assessment
  - Multiple approaches to content, process, and product
  - Student centered
  - A blend of whole-class, group, and individualized instruction
  - Students and teachers learning together

- ◆ The essentials of differentiated instruction
  - A climate that is respectful of individual differences and needs
  - Preassessment to form flexible groups
  - Multiple opportunities to provide practice and gain success with the new skills/knowledge
  - Instruction that is mildly uncomfortable but not frustrating
  - Students know and understand standards of quality and how to self-assess
  - Students understand where they are in relation to the state standards, benchmarks and indicators
  - Students are accountable for their own growth

Three Items Determine Differentiation

Readiness	Interest	Learning Styles
Concrete to abstract	Interest Surveys	Learning Style Inventories
Simple to complex	I-Search	"Intelligence" Preferences
Single facet to multi facet	Group Investigations	Cultural Preferences
Small leap to great leap	Design a Day	Gender-Based Preferences
Structured to open ended	Jigsaw	Combined Preferences
Dependent to independent	Literature Circles	Flexible Grouping
Slow to fast	Negotiated Criteria	Cubing
Scaffolding		

- ◆ Role of the Teacher
  - Organizers of learning activities vs. dispensers of knowledge
  - Directors of orchestras
  - Teacher as coach
  - Creator of lessons that require critical and creative thinking
  - Creators of activities that are a balance of teacher assigned and student selected

Three Areas You Can Differentiate in the Classroom

Content	Process	Product
The level of depth and complexity of the subject matter	*The application of knowledge, skills, and understanding*	*The degree of quality and level of expertise*
♦ Teach for the Big Ideas ♦ Compact the Curriculum ♦ Use varied text and resource materials ♦ Use learning contracts ♦ Teach mini lessons ♦ Vary support (audio, organizers, highlighted materials, peer and adult mentors) ♦ Provide capsules of key ideas	♦ Learning logs ♦ Journals ♦ Graphic organizers ♦ Creative problem solving ♦ Cubing ♦ Learning centers ♦ Interest groups ♦ Learning contracts ♦ Literature circles ♦ Role playing ♦ Think/Pair/Share ♦ Jigsaw ♦ Mind mapping ♦ Tiered projects ♦ Interactive journals	♦ Interactive journals ♦ Identify the goal/standards of the project ♦ Identify one or more formats for the end product ♦ Determine expectations for quality ♦ Decide and plan for the scaffolding you will need to build success ♦ Clearly explain expectations to the learners ♦ Differentiate based on readiness, interests or learning style ♦ Coach for success

Look through these strategies and find the one that works best for you as a teacher or that fits your students and their needs. There are many different ways to differentiate in the classroom. You have to find the one that works best for all those involved and that will produce the results your SMART goal seeks. *Differentiated Instruction* (p. 105) is a chart of differentiated instruction.

Issue: You were not able to get to all the content standards you wanted to cover and find yourself always running out of time.

Possible adjustment in the classroom: Compacting the curriculum

Compacting the curriculum involves taking what you usually teach and fitting it into a shorter time span, using the idea of what students already know and what is most important to learn, building understanding more quickly.

♦ What is compacting?

• Compacting encourages teachers to assess students before beginning instruction.

- Instruction is then planned accordingly—students who do well on the preassessment should not have to continue work on what they already know, but should be learning new things.

♦ Three stages to compacting

1. What the students already know (and evidence for that conclusion)

2. What the preassessment indicates the student does *not* know about the topic or the skill (and plans for how the student will learn these things)

3. A plan for meaningful and challenging use of time that the student will buy into because he or she already knows much of the topic or skill

♦ Tips for Compacting

- Compacting by instructional unit is best. A "unit" generally refers to an instructional period that revolves around a theme, chronological time period, or a set of academic objectives.

- Compacting should be explained in simple terms to all students. Among the points you should touch on are pretests, the fact that some students may already know the material being tested, and that exciting learning activities exist for students who have already mastered the material.

- You must have a clear understanding of your curricular objectives (pacing guide) and a knowledge of which students have already mastered those objectives (short-cycle assessments) or are capable of mastering them in less time.

- You can set up "student stations," consisting of a desk or table with two or three chairs for independent study or free reading. A small, comfortable library corner or special learning or interest centers also can be established.

- Try starting with a small group of students and not the entire class. This process will take some time and organization so become committed to trying to work with a group who really needs the process first. By not trying this with all students, you reduce the stress and challenges you might encounter if you tried to do too much in the beginning of the process.

Compacting the curriculum begins with a focus on student readiness and ends with an emphasis on student interest. The good thing is that you have already pretested using the short-cycle assessment. This data will provide you with an idea of where your students are and to where they can go. You can use this data to establish what it is you should and should not compact.

Issue: I need to go back and reteach several groups of students certain standards they did not master on the short-cycle assessment without slowing the entire class down.

Possible adjustment in the classroom: Provide flexible grouping of students using tiered lessons when necessary.

Using the Non-Mastery Report you can get a good idea which students still need to master certain standards. With this report in mind, you can set up flexible groups to go back and reteach the standard. For instance, let's say you are trying to teach students the following science standard:

Explain that some processes involved in the rock cycle are directly related to thermal energy and forces in the mantle that drive plate motions.

Students have to understand what a rock cycle is, what thermal energy is, and what plate motions are and synthesize that knowledge so as to understand the standard. If some students in the class have demonstrated that they do not understand any or even some of these skills, those skills will need to be taught again before moving on to a mastery level. Rather than subjecting the entire class to this reteaching, you can put those who do not have the concepts into a group and review them. In the meantime the rest of the class can begin to cover the standard in much greater depth. By the end of the lesson the groups will be at very different depths of understanding, but will be able to master the basic concept as laid out by the Content Standard.

The key to this concept is having tiered lessons. Do not feel you need to change daily instruction; instead, develop alternative products you think will be of interest to students and that will match their skill level. This means different groups will be doing different things but ending up at the same place. The tiered lesson may allow different groups to work at different paces, but again, the idea is that they will still end up with the same mastery they need to understand the standard.

Issue: My special education students never seem to be able to catch up with the rest of the class.

Possible adjustment in the classroom: Teach specific compensation strategies to these students while concentrating on the "Big Ideas" in the standards.

A recurring frustration for teachers who have special education students in their classrooms is trying to "close the gap" while virtually swimming upstream. This has always been a problem, but add to that the age of Content Standards and the issue really gets complicated. While we cannot solve this problem here, we can offer a few suggestions or ways to think about things "outside the box."

Consider the idea that perhaps our time would be better spent teaching these students compensation techniques and strategies rather than trying to cram 3 years worth of learning into 9 months. Teaching these students how to glean meaning from a newspaper written at an eighth grade level may be a more important life skill for them to learn than what sound the letters "gh" may make. Also, these compensation techniques are ones that the student can transfer to a testing situation, thereby alleviating confusion and frustration. For those of you not familiar with compensation strategies, see *Compensation Strategies for Special Education Students* on page 172.

The next issue for the special education students is their right to learn the standards at their grade level. Think about it this way: If a student is never exposed to grade-level material and then is suddenly given an assessment on grade level, what chance does that student have to be successful? Talk about setting a student up to fail. We believe that special education students should be exposed to grade-level-appropriate material at least half the time, with the other half being devoted to strengthening their weak areas of learning. This time spent on grade-level material could be spent by teaching compensation strategies, compacting the curriculum and teaching the big ideas, or with other types of interventions and modifications such as extended time, and visual and auditory accommodations. Let's examine a practical example of this.

Suppose you have a fifth grade student who is reading at a second grade level. Now, at the fifth grade level the standard in language arts for setting goes something like this:

Describe how the setting of a story influences the plot of the story.

If you only teach that student using second grade material, it is very likely that the only thing they will be asked to do with regard to setting is to identify it—a grade 2 standard. Thus, whether you mean to or not, you are actually limiting that student in their learning. A better thing to do is to provide the student with a reading selection on their instructional level—grade 2—but then provide them with discussion questions meant to teach the standard.

Another point to consider is whatever modifications and accommodations are listed on a student's Individualized Education Plan (IEP) also should be followed on a student's short-cycle assessment. If a student's IEP states that the student needs to have the tests read to him or her, then they should be read to the student on the short-cycle assessments.

One last point to consider in regard to special education. Although we never advocate that students be set up to fail, we will pass on a thought that was shared with us during a somewhat heated debate on this topic. Math teachers were debating whether or not all students should be required to take Algebra. Some of the teachers were presenting the argument that many students do not have the intellectual capacity to fully understand Algebra even though they were quick to concede that Algebra was a major part of the state test. After much debate one of the teachers, who up until this time had been fairly quiet, stood up and made the following statement: "Someone who has taken Algebra and failed Algebra still knows more about Algebra than someone who has never taken it." This same philosophy holds true for special education students and the Content Standards. If these students are taught the standards and there is even a small degree of learning, they will know more than if they were never taught the standards at all.

Issue: My advanced students seem bored having to wait for the rest of the class to catch up with them.

Possible adjustment in the classroom: Alternative assessments such as performance-based assessments, and independent study assignments can be provided.

For some of your more advanced students, offering alternative assessments such as performance-based assessments can not only be motivating, but can provide you with more information than a high grade on a regular assessment can. These students need to think of assessment as more than a simple pencil-to-paper assessment and they themselves may come up with creative ways to present what they have learned. These alternative assessments could take several forms:

- A defense of a paper they have written or read
- A presentation on a specific topic or standard
- A PowerPoint summarizing learning that has taken place
- A demonstration of learning a specific standard
- A Q&A session defending their knowledge of a standard
- A short skit on a given topic or standard

The key to alternative assessment is to make the grading of the performance less subjective and more objective. This will give you the most information.

How to Ensure Rubrics are Objective

- Be as specific as you can be in the rubric.
- Anchor grading if you have the opportunity.
  - Have a couple of people, including students in the class, fill out rubrics.
  - Self-assessments can be done as well.
- Write many comments on the actual rubric so that students are clear why you marked what you did.
- Link the descriptions to specific indicators when possible.
- If something is more valued or weighed more heavily in the grading than something else, make sure that is clear.

For a blank form you can use to create an objective rubric with which to evaluate performance-based assessments, see *Rubric* on page 173.

Independent study as a form of alternative assessment is also an option. If students appear to be working ahead of the rest of the class, provide them with the opportunity to go further in-depth independently, stretching the boundaries of the standard. Students will set their own pace and decide how deeply they will pursue the standard. Hopefully, they will challenge themselves with this inquiry. Many accelerated students like to learn independently because it allows them to have more choice in what they are learning and take responsibility for their own education. A learning contract is a useful tool when working with a student on an independent study. Make sure the contract is one in which the student himself can have a lot of input. For a blank learning contract to get you started, see *Project Contract* on page 174.

The Short of Making Adjustments in the Classroom

The key to making adjustments in the classroom is knowing when those adjustments will be in the best interest of your students and yourself. Some key points to remember when making adjustments are as follows:

- Identify a need from the short-cycle assessment data analysis. Always use concrete data to drive your instructional decisions.

- Stick with one, maybe two improvements you want to make. That way you will not be overwhelmed.

- Set a specific goal of improvement you wish to see following the SMART goals.

- Make sure the goals are measurable so you can monitor growth.

- Stay within the risk area of the learning circle. Doing too much too fast might cause your students to end up in the danger area—not a good place for you or your students.

- Remember that change is not an easy thing. If you have a support group such as a Critical Friends Group (CFG), a Professional Learning Community, or even a colleague(s) you can bounce ideas off of, this will help with the process.

Epilogue:
Where to Go From Here?

Aim for success, not perfection. Never give up your right to be wrong, because then you will lose the ability to learn new things and move forward with your life.

Dr. David M. Burns

The SCORE Process

Let's review the steps you have covered so far:

- ◆ Step 1: Understanding of State Standards (Chapter 3)
- ◆ Step 2: Understanding of the State Assessment (Chapter 4)
- ◆ Step 3: Development of Pacing Guide (Chapter 5)
- ◆ Step 4: Design Assessment to Standards (Chapter 7)
- ◆ Step 5: Administer Assessment (Chapter 8)
- ◆ Step 6: Data Analysis of Assessment (Chapter 9)
- ◆ Step 7: Data-Based Instructional Adjustments (Chapter 10)

That brings us to the last step in this cycle but by far not the last step in the process:

- ◆ Step 8: Curriculum Mapping.

What this means for you and your school is this: After you get a year of the SCORE Process under your belt, you need to step back and look at the big picture. Did your pacing guide work the way you set it up or do you need to reevaluate it? Did you like the questions on your short-cycle assessments or would you like to revise some of them? What about your classroom instruction is going to be different now that you have learned to make adjustments in the classroom?

Curriculum mapping is a detailed way of setting up the year with the knowledge you learned from the previous year of going through the SCORE Process. You know the old saying, "If I knew then what I know now, things would be very different." Here is your chance to put this into practice. This next year is simply going to be a repeat of the SCORE cycle from before only now you clearly understand the state standards and the state assessment so these can be eliminated from the cycle (Figure E-1).

**Figure E-1 Step 8 of the SCORE Process:
Curriculum Mapping**

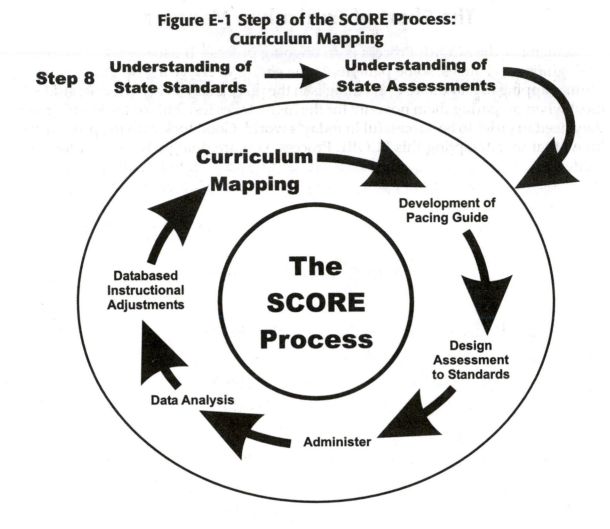

Curriculum mapping is going to specifically get into the what, how, and when of the curriculum. It is the details behind the data-based instructional adjustments. Many schools do curriculum mapping before they do anything else. We think it makes more sense to do curriculum mapping after you have analyzed the data from your short-cycle assessments.

The most important aspect to remember about the SCORE Process is that this cycle never becomes set in stone. Because learning is an ongoing process, you will continue to learn how to make adjustments in the classroom, write better test questions, and overall understand the pace of the year better. You will continue to go through the SCORE Process year after year, improving what you have done. Know that you are going to make mistakes and it is the learning from those mistakes that give you the professional development that shapes you into a better teacher.

The Short of Curriculum Mapping

Remember the SCORE Process is an ongoing process. It usually takes 3 years to see significant changes, so be patient. At the end of every year, revisit your curriculum mapping to make sure everything is in the place that will benefit your students most when preparing them not only for the high-stakes test, but for the learning that they need in order to be successful in today's world. Good luck with the process and know that by attempting this SCORE Process, you are doing what is best for your students.

Part II

Blueprints
for the Process

This section is designed to give you the blueprints needed to construct the SCORE Process. Here you will find activities, blank forms, handouts, and anything else needed for you to follow the steps that have been laid out for you in the various chapters.

1. Teaching to the Test
2. Testing Twice
3. Figuring Out Which SCORE Model Works Best for You
4. Bloom's Taxonomy Key Words
5. The Taxonomy Table
6. Curriculum Pacing Guide for the SCORE Process
7. Standard to Question
8. Response Grid Question Practice
9. Writing Your Own Rubric
10. Alaska's 6-Point Rubric
11. Blank Rubrics
12. What *Not* to Write
13. Goldilocks and the Six Levels of Bloom's Taxonomy
14. How to Write a Multiple-Choice Question
15. Questions Conversion Chart
16. Revising and Editing Worksheet #1
17. Revising and Editing Worksheet #2
18. Assessment Checklist
19. Pacing Guide Confirmation
20. Writing Assessment Checklist
21. Reading Assessment Checklist
22. General Assessment Checklist
23. Do Not Disturb Sign
24. Directions to Read to Students
25. Assessment Directions Sheet
26. Class Profile Graph
27. Class Item Analysis Graph
28. Non-Mastery Report
29. Individual Assessment Reflection
30. Group Data Analysis for Assessment #1
31. Group Data Analysis for Assessment #2
32. Group Data Analysis for Assessment #3

33. Group Data Analysis for Assessment #4
34. How Did You Learn What Was Taught?
35. SMART Goals
36. Differentiated Instruction
37. Compensation Strategies for Special Education Students
38. Rubric
39. Project Contract

Teaching to the Test

"Teaching to the Test" has certainly gotten a bad rap in the educational world. Teachers usually utter these words with disdain in their voices and displeasure on their faces. After all, they say, preparing the students for the high-stakes state test is nothing more than "teaching to the test" (don't forget to add the negative tone and grumpy face!). If we teach to the test, apparently, we are not doing our jobs. Is this the absolute truth?

To "stretch" your way of thinking with regard to "teaching to the test," you will need to imagine yourself in the following situations and answer the questions accordingly:

♦ You are the coach of a high school football team. You are preparing your players for the big rivalry game on Friday night. You know the other team is going to pass the ball a lot. You also know that opponents have scored a lot of points by running the ball against your team's defensive line. To best prepare your players for the game, you should spend the most time working on

   A. your passing offense and your running defense.

   B. your running offense and your passing defense.

   C. your kicking game.

   D. your punt return.

♦ You are 16 years old and getting ready to take your driver's test on Saturday. You know there will be a written test as well as an actual driving test. You will prepare for your driver's test by

   A. learning the rules of the road only.

   B. practicing driving only.

   C. studying how to best hail a cab in heavy traffic.

   D. learning the rules of driving, as well as spending hours practicing actual driving.

♦ You are a college student majoring in education. You are in your senior year, and will have to take the State Teacher Examination at the end of the semester. In preparation for the test, you have taken a course entitled, "Strategies for Ensuring Success on the State Teacher Examination." You go to the class for the entire semester and learn how to create your own portfolio. How do you feel when the time comes to take the test? Why do you feel that way? Did the instructor do his job?

♦ You are sitting in a college graduate class. The professor is talking on and on about something completely unrelated to the context of the course.

This goes on for several minutes before the somewhat hyperactive and extremely literal guy in the front row raises his hand. The professor stops and asks the man to ask his question. It is the question everyone in the room is dying to ask: "Is this going to be on the test?" Why didn't the man ask this question instead: "Could you please tell us some more stories like this one?" Is it because

A. he doesn't really like the professor?

B. he doesn't want to waste his time on irrelevant information?

C. he's already heard the story?

D. he wants to learn what will be useful to him in the final assessment of the material?

Let's talk about the next-to-last scenario. Did you learn anything? If you actually learned to create a portfolio, you did. Was it valuable? Certainly. Was it aligned to the assessment you were going to take? Absolutely not. What about the instructor? Let's say that your instructor knew exactly what the State Teacher Examination was about, but your instructor decided not to teach you what was going to be on this "high-stakes" test (at least to you it is "high-stakes"). Would you appreciate your instructor's decision? Would you feel your instructor was doing his or her job?

All of the situations described above seem like common sense. Of course a coach would prepare the team for the talent they will face in the next athletic contest. Of course you would prepare for a driver's test by learning what was going to be on the written test, as well as learning what was going to be on the performance test. Of course you would expect the instructor in the State Teacher Examination Prep Class to teach you the things you need to know to be successful on that test. And of course you would want your professor to teach you the information you need to know to be successful on the final assessment. How many times in college, when your professor was going off on another tangent concerning his great abilities, did you think to yourself, "Why do I need to know this if it's not going to be on the test?" In other words, you would want the instructor to "teach to the test"! Ahhh, that's a different way of thinking about it, isn't it?

Of course, when we say "teach to the test" we are talking about teaching the skills necessary to be successful on the test. You would not want a 16-year-old to only memorize the answers to the actual written driver's test with little or no thought as to what it means. Competent drivers need to be able to apply knowledge of yielding and switching lanes to be safe on the road. Students need to learn the content and be able to show that they have "enduring understanding" of that content.

To put it simply: if you as an educator, know what is going to be on the "high-stakes" test, and you purposefully do not prepare your students to be successful on that test, are you doing your job? Just something to think about…

Testing Twice

Directions: Put these steps in chronological order, numbering from 1 to 10, 1 being the first step, 10 being the last. Time yourself to see how quickly you can complete the list correctly.

Brushing Your Teeth

_____Tap the toothbrush to get any excess water off.

_____Spit out any excess toothpaste.

_____Run the toothbrush under the faucet to get it wet.

_____Rinse your mouth with water.

_____Take the top off of the toothpaste.

_____Return the toothbrush and toothpaste to the drawer.

_____Get your toothbrush and toothpaste out of the drawer.

_____Put a small amount of toothpaste on your brush.

_____Brush your teeth.

_____Rinse the sink of any toothpaste or spit.

Directions: Put these steps in chronological order, numbering from 1 to 10, 1 being the first step, 10 being the last. Time yourself to see how quickly you can complete the list correctly.

Making a Snowman

_____Roll some snow into a medium-size snowball.

_____Put a scarf and hat on the top snowball.

_____Roll some snow into a large snowball.

_____Put eyes, a nose, and a mouth on the top snowball.

_____Wait until you have a huge snowfall—at least 3 inches.

_____Place the small snowball on top of the medium one.

_____Place the medium-size snowball on top of the large one.

_____Pick a level place to build your snowman.

_____Name your snowman and enjoy his company!

_____Roll some snow into a small snowball.

Did your time improve any on the second test? Consider the fact that the second test was designed to take longer because the responses have to be more carefully read. If your time did improve, why do you suppose this is? Might it be because you were more familiar with the format?

Answer Keys

Brushing Your Teeth

8   Tap the toothbrush to get any excess water off.

6   Spit out any excess toothpaste.

2   Run the toothbrush under the faucet to get it wet.

7   Rinse your mouth with water.

3   Take the top off of the toothpaste.

10   Return the toothbrush and toothpaste to the drawer.

1   Get your toothbrush and toothpaste out of the drawer.

4   Put a small amount of toothpaste on your brush.

5   Brush your teeth.

9   Rinse the sink of any toothpaste or spit.

Making a Snowman

4   Roll some snow into a medium-size snowball.

9   Put a scarf and hat on the top snowball.

3   Roll some snow into a large snowball.

8   Put eyes, a nose, and a mouth on the top snowball.

1   Wait until you have a huge snowfall—at least 3 inches.

7   Place the small snowball on top of the medium one.

5   Place the medium-size snowball on top of the large one.

2   Pick a level place to build your snowman.

10   Name your snowman and enjoy his company!

6   Roll some snow into a small snowball.

Figuring Out Which SCORE Model Works Best for You

How are your grading periods divided up? (6 weeks, 9 weeks) _____

Rate all of the following on a scale from 1 to 10. Use any number within that range but do not use fractions or anything above or below it.

How often do you feel the students need to review the content standards and their understanding of them in an assessment form?

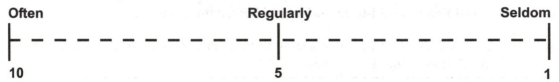

If you were to receive information on a student before the grading period, how influential would that be in guiding your instruction?

On a scale from 1 to 10, 10 being low and 1 being high, how much endurance do your students have for taking tests.

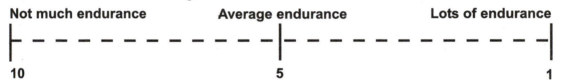

How much class time do you need to cover all of the standards required by the state assessment?

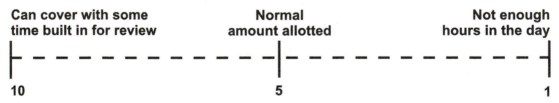

How well did your school do on the state assessment the year before, 10 being poorly, 1 being advanced in all subject areas?

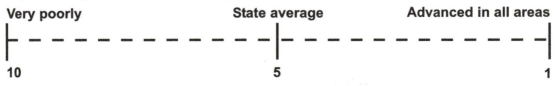

Total score _____

50–45	Should have both pre- and postassessments for each grading period.
44–40	Should have at least one assessment a grading period with a practice test at the beginning of the school year.
39–25	Should have an assessment every grading period.
24–15	Should have a mid-term and a final before the state test.
14–5	Should have a mid-term assessment to determine where students mastery is in relation to the state standards.

Bloom's Taxonomy Key Words

Knowledge	choose, define, find, how, identify, label, list, locate, name, omit, recall, recognize, select, show, spell, tell, what, when, where, which, who, why
Comprehension	add, compare, describe, distinguish, explain, express, extend, illustrate, outline, paraphrase, relate, rephrase, summarize, translate, understand
Application	answer, apply, build, choose, conduct, construct, demonstrate, develop, experiment with, illustrate, interview, make use of, model, organize, plan, present, produce, respond, solve
Analysis	analyze, assumption, categorize, classify, compare and contrast, conclusion, deduce, discover, dissect, distinguish, edit, examine, explain, function, infer, inspect, motive, reason, test for, validate
Synthesis	build, change, combine, compile, compose, construct, create, design, develop, discuss, estimate, formulate, hypothesize, imagine, integrate, invent, make up, modify, originate, organize, plan, predict, propose, rearrange, revise, suppose, theorize
Evaluation	appraise, assess, award, conclude, criticize, debate, defend, determine, disprove, evaluate, give opinion, interpret, justify, judge, influence, prioritize, prove, recommend, support, verify

The Taxonomy Table

Analyze the content standards looking at the verb and determining the level of the grade-level indicator.

Knowledge	Comprehension	Application	Analysis	Synthesis	Evaluate

Curriculum Pacing Guide for the Score Process

District _____   Grade Level _____   Subject Area _____

Grading Period 1	Grading Period 2	Grading Period 3	Grading Period 4

Standard to Question

Place a standard here:

Change the standard to a single question with the addition of only a few words:

Now break the question into a two-, three-, or four-part constructed response depending on what format your state assessment follows:

Part A:

Part B:

Part C:

Part D:

Now try turning it into a multiple-choice question:

a.

b.

c.

d.

Response Grid Question Practice

Remember that a response grid question needs to require students to calculate a correct numerical answer.

Try writing a response grid question at a knowledge level:

Questions that require recall and/or basic recognition

   Cue words: choose, find, list, locate, memorize, name, outline, recite, repeat

Try writing a response grid question at a comprehension level:

Questions that require interpretation of main ideas or summarization

   Cue words: approximate, articulate, calculate, characterize, relate, retell, subtract, summarize, translate, understand

Try writing a response grid question at an application level:

Questions that take concrete situations and enable problem solving

   Cue words: acquire, action, answer, draw, illustrate, manipulate, organize, prepare, perform, predict present, produce, solve

Try writing a response grid question at an analysis level:
Questions that break down a concept or idea into parts and show relation-ships among the parts.

> *Cue words: analyze, ask, categorize, chart, compare, contrast, correlate, in-quire, infer, reason, sequence, distinguish*

Try writing a response grid question at a synthesis level:
Questions that bring together parts to form a new whole

> *Cue words: propose, formulate, plan, create, imagine, speculate, compose, design, construct*

Try writing a response grid question at an evaluation level:
Questions that judge the value of material for a given purpose using a specific set of criteria.

> *Cue words: compare, pros/cons, judge, evaluate, assess, decide, rate, con-vince, predict, criticize, value*

Writing Your Own Rubric

Step 1: Decide the number of points the writing response is worth.

- ♦ This should model what the state assessment uses to get students used to their system.

Step 2: Provide several descriptors for each point.

- ♦ Each category should have several skills being evaluated.
  - • This breakdown allows the evaluation to be objective.
  - • This does not put too much weight on any one skill.
- ♦ These should be describing specific skills.

Step 3: Make sure descriptors are specific and not vague.

- ♦ You should be able to apply this phrase to each descriptor "What does it look like?"
- ♦ Use specific numbers or a range if the category lends itself to it.
  - • Ex: Provides three examples, is 15–20 minutes in length, has 7 or fewer spelling mistakes.
- ♦ Don't over explain or the rubric might become confusing or you might handcuff yourself while grading.
  - • There needs to be some wiggle room when grading.

Step 4: Use a tiered system to define the descriptors.

- ♦ Each descriptor should have a matching descriptor at each level.
  - • In other words the skill being assessed should be described on an excellent, good, and needs improvement level.
  - • If you have four descriptors at the top level, there should be four matching descriptors at all the other levels.
- ♦ Make sure each level is realistic.
  - • The top level should have high expectations.
  - • The bottom levels should be honest and aligned to performance.

Step 5: Test the rubric with your students.

- ♦ Check each category going through the tiers to be sure it flows and makes sense.
- ♦ Practice grading an old essay or a rough draft to see how practical it is.
- ♦ Have students or another teacher look it over for any mistakes they might find.
- ♦ If you discover mistakes while grading, take note of them and change them for next time.

Alaska's 6-Point Rubric

General Communication Scoring Guide

	Message is	Delivery is	Information	Language Structure	Pronunciation	Vocabluary
6	easily understood in its entirety	effortless and smooth	expands on all relevant information	employs complex structures and speech; demonstrates a sophistication beyond that which has been studied	approximates native speech	is used accurately with creative variety
5	comprehensible in its entirety with a few minor flaws	has no unnatural pauses; sounds like natural speech	includes all relevant information	employees consistent and accurate use of structures; may contain a few minor errors that don't interfere with the communication	is mostly correct with only minor flaws	is varied and accurate
4	generally comprehensible	fairly smooth with a few unnatural pauses; slight choppiness and/or occasional error in information	includes most relevant information	generally uses correct structures with some errors	influenced by first language	is appropriate
3	somewhat comprehensible	occasionally halting and fragmentary with some unnatural pauses, choppiness, or inappropriate intonation	includes a fair amount of relevant information; may include contradictions, informational gaps, or redundancies	demonstrates an inconsistent use of correct structures	shows strong influence from first language	is simple with some inappropriate use
2	difficult to understand	very halting and fragmentary with many unnatural pauses; speech sounds mechanical	little relevant information is presented	shows many errors in use of structure	is dominated by first language	is limited or incorrect
1	incomprehensible	very halting and fragmentary with excessive unnatural pauses	vague or confusing information is presented	has no apparent understanding of structures	interferes with comprehension	is very poor or inaccurate for topic; first language words may be used; speaker may create a target language form from first language

Adapted from Second Language Elementary, Oregon Department of Education, February, 1995

Blank Rubrics

Score Point	Score Point Description
4	The written response:
3	The written response:
2	The written response:
1	The written response:
0	The written response:

Score Point	Score Point Description
6	The written response:
5	The written response:
4	The written response:
3	The written response:
2	The written response:
1	The written response:
0	The written response:

What *Not* to Write

Multiple Choice:

Not

Which element is represented by the symbol Ca?

    A. Chlorine

    B. Calcium

    C. Carbonate

    D. Carbon

- This question is lower level and requires recall of memorized facts.

But

Partial Periodic Table of Elements

1 H							**2 He**
3 Li	**4 Be**		**5 B**	**6 C**	**7 N**	**8 O**	**9 F**	**10 Ne**

Both hydrogen gas and helium gas are lighter than air. Why is helium used to lift blimps instead of hydrogen?

    A. Hydrogen has a tendency to lose an electron, decreasing lift.

    B. Helium is more chemically stable than hydrogen and will not burn.

    C. Hydrogen has less lifting force than helium because it has less mass.

    D. Helium has more lifting force than hydrogen because it has more electrons.

- This question requires reading, interpreting, and drawing conclusions from information in a chart.

Constructed Response:

Not

What effect did the case *Brown vs. Board of Education of Topeka* have on public education today?

- This question relies on prior knowledge. Also, this is meant to be a two-point question, but the question does not have *two* clear parts. How will it be scored?

But

In the landmark case *Brown vs. Board of Education of Topeka* (1954), the U.S. Supreme Court ruled that racial segregation in public schools was unconstitutional. In a ruling the next year, the Supreme Court ordered that schools must proceed with integration. Describe one effect these rulings have had on public education today. Evaluate whether you think the rulings were good or bad, and explain.

- ♦ This question requires the student to analyze a situation. It is also clear about what is expected: one point for an effect and one point for an evaluation.

Multiple Choice:

Not

Work the following problem:

$6 \times 7 =$

A. 36

B. 42

C. 32

- • This question is lower level and requires recall of a memorized fact.

But

When John was asked to work the problem $6 \times 7 =$ ___, he worked it the following way:

$6 + 6 + 6 + 6 + 6 + 6 + 6 = 42$

Sam worked it this way:

$6 \times 7 = 42$

Both ways are correct. Choose the reason why they are both right.

A. 6×7 means 6 added up 6 times.

B. They both produce the answer 42.

C. They both have the numeral 6 in the problem.

- • This question requires the student to analyze a situation and make a determination based on that analysis.

Constructed Response:

Not

Write the names of the following shapes.

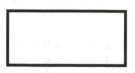  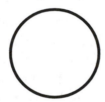 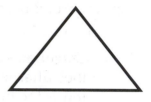

_____   _____   _____   _____

♦ This question is lower level because it requires memorization. Also, it is demonstrating mastery of one skill—shape identification—four times.

But

Look at the figures below. Label each figure. How are the figures alike? How are they different? Sort the figures and label how you sorted.

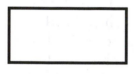 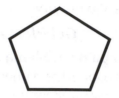  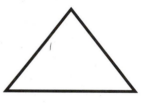

_____   _____   _____   _____

Label: _____

Alike: _____

Different: _____

I sorted by: _____

♦ This question has four separate skills and requires the student to analyze and evaluate.

Goldilocks and the Six Levels of Bloom's Taxonomy

Most of us know the story of *Goldilocks and the Three Bears* but just to be sure, here is a condensed version of the story to use to write six multiple choice questions, one at each level of Bloom's Taxonomy.

Goldilocks and the Three Bears

1. Three bears, Papa Bear, Mama Bear, and Baby Bear had just sat down to eat their afternoon porridge. When they went to eat it, all three of them agreed it was too hot. Mama Bear suggested going on a walk to give the porridge time to cool off. Papa Bear and Baby Bear agreed, so they left their house to go on the walk.

2. In the meantime, a young girl by the name of Goldilocks had been walking through the forest on her way to her grandmother's house. She had been walking a long way and was very hungry and tired. She spotted the Bear's house and decided to see if she could stop to rest there. When she knocked on the door, it opened so she decided to go inside. She did not find anyone inside but she did see the three bowls of porridge.

3. She was so hungry that she could not resist taking a taste of the delicious-looking food. She tasted Papa Bear's and declared, "This porridge is too hot." She tried Mama Bear's bowl and found that it was too cold. There was one last bowl and when she tasted it, the porridge was just right. She couldn't control herself and ate the entire bowl in a matter of minutes.

4. After finishing her meal, Goldilocks found herself becoming very tired. She figured if she could find a place to lay down for just a few minutes she could recharge her battery. She located a room with three beds in it. She lay down in the first one, which was Papa Bear's. She was only in it a few moments before she determined it was too hard. The next bed, Mama Bear's, looked a lot softer and as Goldilocks lay down on it, she sunk into it. It was too soft so she got out of it and tried the final bed, Baby Bear's. This bed was just right, so right that she found herself immediately falling asleep.

5. The Three Bears returned from their walk, looking forward to eating the delicious porridge that was awaiting them. When they sat down to eat, they noticed something was wrong. "Hey, someone's been eating my porridge!" Papa Bear announced. Mama Bear noticed that her porridge had been eaten from as well. Baby Bear looked into his empty bowl and cried, "Someone's been eating my porridge and it's all gone."

6. The Bears became alarmed that someone was in the house. They searched all over, looking for the intruder. When they went into the bedroom, Papa Bear noticed his bed was messed up. Mama Bear also noticed that her bed was messy, saying, "Someone's been sleeping in my bed." Baby Bear went

over and pointed to his bed. "Someone's been sleeping in my bed and she's still there!"

7. Goldilocks heard Baby Bear shouting, woke up, and ran out of the house leaving the three Bears behind.

Write a knowledge level question:

Write a comprehension level question:

Write an application level question:

Write an analysis level question:

Write a synthesis question:

Write an evaluation question:

Perhaps the most difficult question to write is a multiple-choice, higher-level question. We have developed a three-step process to help with this task. The three steps are:

1. Think of the question that you want to ask. Think of it as a constructed response question. Simply ask the question. It does not matter at this time how many parts there is to the question, or even what you are asking the student to do. Block those things from your mind and write the question. For example, if the standard is…

   Describe how the setting of a story influences the plot of the story.

   …and you had the student read the story, *Goldilocks and the Three Bears*, your question might be: "How would the plot change if the setting of the story were changed to a busy city instead of a quiet forest and why would that cause it to change?"

2. Think of a correct answer for that question. If the question has more than one correct answer, think of an answer that you would consider to be exemplary. Write that answer down. You now have your question and the correct answer choice. For example, using the question for *Goldilocks* mentioned above, a correct answer might be "Goldilocks might have failed to get into the Bear's home because people in the city are more likely to lock their doors."

3. Now, comes the hard part—the distracters. You will need to write two to three distracters, or the other answer choices, for your question. The distracters need to sound plausible, yet incorrect. If your question has two parts, then an easy way to do this is to include the correct answer for one part of the distracter, and the incorrect answer for the second part. Then, switch that around and you have two incorrect distracters. For example, the distracters for our *Goldilocks* question might be:

A. Goldilocks might have failed to get into the Bear's home because people in the city are more likely to keep their doors unlocked.

B. Goldilocks might have been able to enter the Bear's home easily because people in the city are more likely to lock their doors.

Now, the final distracter is always the most difficult to write. This is where we, as teachers, tend to favor the "goofy," far out answers. Because the state tests do not have "goofy" answer choices, we ask that you write a plausible answer choice for your distracter. An example of a third distracter for this question might be:

C. Goldilocks might have failed to eat the porridge as people in the city are more likely to have boxed cereal than porridge.

The final question, put altogether, reads like this:

How would the plot change if the setting of the story were changed to a busy city instead of a quiet forest and why would that cause it to change?

A. Goldilocks might have failed to get into the Bear's home because people in the city are more likely to keep their doors unlocked.

B. Goldilocks might have been able to enter the Bear's home easily because people in the city are more likely to lock their doors.

C. Goldilocks might have failed to eat the porridge as people in the city are more likely to have boxed cereal than porridge.

D. Goldilocks might have failed to get into the Bear's home because people in the city are more likely to lock their doors.

At this point in the question writing process, we hear two arguments. The first is that the way the first two distracters are written indicates that we are merely trying to "trick" the student. That is one way of looking at it. A different way of viewing this is to think that we are requiring the students to be very careful readers—not a bad thing to be. The second argument has to do with distracter C. This is where someone will inevitably argue that the choice is possible—that the Bears might indeed have had boxed cereal instead of porridge. If you think carefully, however, even if the food was boxed cereal and not porridge, the plot would not change. Ahhh…

Just for argument's sake, let's say that the third distracter was something that *could* have happened, but not likely to happen, and that it would have changed the plot in some way. For example, if the answer choice were, "Goldilocks might have failed to get into the Bear's home because they may have never left because city people do not take walks." In a case like this, a simple way to solve this problem is to add the sentence, "Choose the best answer.", or "Choose the most likely answer." to the end of the question. This will cause the student to have to move into the critical thinking part of their brains as they will have to analyze, synthesize, and evaluate.

So, to sum it up, think of the question and write it down. Think of the answer and write it down. Think of the distracters and write them down. For a template regarding writing multiple-choice questions see *How to Write a Multiple Choice Question* on page 145.

How to Write a Multiple-Choice Question

Writing a multiple-choice question is easy once you know the formula. It doesn't matter if the question is a lower-level recall question, or higher-level thinking question, the formula is the same. Just follow these three easy steps.

1. Write the question.

    _____

    _____

    _____

2. Write the correct answer.

    _____

    _____

    _____

3. Write the three distracters.

    A. _____

    _____

    B. _____

    _____

    C. _____

    _____

Now, put them all together and you have a multiple choice question. Remember to vary under which letter you put the correct answer.

Questions Conversion Chart

You can use the released tests found on your state's department of education website to determine the number and types of questions on your state assessment. (It is recommended that you use two of the tests for your subject area to make sure the average is consistent but it is not necessary.)

Total number of questions on the state   carry # down through
assessment   _____   this column

Number of multiple choice questions   _____ ÷ _____ × 20 = _____ questions

Number of constructed response
questions (____ pts.)   _____ ÷ _____ × 20 = _____ questions

Number of constructed response
questions (____ pts.)   _____ ÷ _____ × 20 = _____ questions

Number of constructed response
questions (____ pts.)   _____ ÷ _____ × 20 = _____ questions

Number of response grid questions   _____ ÷ _____ × 20 = _____ questions

Number of written responses   _____ ÷ _____ × 20 = _____ questions

Revising and Editing Worksheet #1

Analyze each question on your assessment and fill out the chart below indicating the question, the standard, the question format (multiple choice, constructed response [including points worth], or response grid), and the level of the question according to Bloom's taxonomy.

Ques.	Standard	MC	CR	RG	WP	Lower Level Ques.			Higher Level Ques.		
						Know.	Comp.	Appl.	Anal.	Synth.	Eval.
1.											
2.											
3.											
4.											
5.											
6.											
7.											
8.											
9.											
10.											
11.											
12.											
13.											
14.											
15.											
16.											
17.											
18.											
19.											
20.											
21.											
22.											
23.											
24.											
25.											
TOTALS											

Revising and Editing Worksheet #2

Grade Level _____ Subject _____ Assessment # _____

Please review your assessment question by question, and fill out the revising and editing checklist below. Pay attention to the Revision Suggestions provided to you. Make your changes directly onto the assessment labeled **Master Revisions.** *Feel free to write notes to the typist when necessary. When you are finished, turn in the checklist and your revised assessment. Thank you.*

Ques. # _____ Standard _____

Level of Bloom's Taxonomy _____

The question fairly assesses the standard.   _____ yes _____ no

   (If no, please rewrite the question.)

The format of the question is correct – Mult. Choice or
Constructed Response   _____ yes _____ no

   (If no, please rewrite the question.)

The graphics, pictures etc. are acceptable.   _____ yes _____ no

   (If no, please explain what needs to be done.)

The answer on the Answer Key is clear and complete.   _____ yes _____ no

   (If no, please correct.)

The space needed to fill out/write the answers is suitable.   _____ yes _____ no

   (If no, please explain what needs to be done.)

Suggestions for Revision:

_____

_____

_____

_____

_____

Do your multiple choice questions have the appropriate number of answer choices? Do your constructed response questions have clear parts assessing different skills? Do your questions assess the level of Bloom's taxonomy on your Taxonomy Table?

Assessment Checklist

Go over the assessment carefully. Use the checklist below to determine if the assessment meets the criteria.

Yes　No

☐☐ The type font is a good size for your students.

☐☐ The format is acceptable: there is enough space for the answers, there are enough lines for the written answers, the lines are big enough with enough room in between them, there are not too many questions on each page, etc.

☐☐ Each question is very clear. If the question is worth 2 points, the question clearly asks for 2 answers. If the question is worth 4 points it clearly asks for a detailed answer.

☐☐ The multiple choice questions have answers that are similar and require the student to think. There are no "off-the-wall" answers that the student can eliminate.

☐☐ The questions involve more than just recalling facts; the students need to be able to think, apply knowledge, and analyze information. There are at least 50% higher level questions.

☐☐ The Directions for Administration and the Answer Key are not ambiguous, but are very clear. There are no "Accept Reasonable Answers". Specific examples are given for acceptable answers. When necessary, examples of unacceptable answers are given.

☐☐ One point is given for each skill. Multiple points are not given for one skill. Ex: Instead of 3 pts. for 3 addition problems, 1 pt. will be given for 3 addition problems.

☐☐ The levels of the questions match your Taxonomy Table.

☐☐ There is a good distribution of multiple choice and constructed response questions that matches the state assessment.

Pacing Guide Confirmation

Take a look at the Academic Content Standards/Grade-Level Indicators that you have placed in the designated area on your Pacing Guide. Write those standards on the chart below and check off whether or not they are assessed on this assessment.

Standard	Assessed on this Assessment	Not Assessed on this Assessment

Look at the standards that you have indicated are not assessed on this assessment. How will each of these indicators be assessed? Design a question or provide a checklist within the assessment to collect the data for the indicator. Write your question/checklist on a question template form, and attach it to the master revision copy of the assessment.

Writing Assessment Checklist

School/District _____ Date _____

Grade _____ Assessment # _____

	Yes	No
Assessment contains one writing prompt.		
Writing prompt covers the writing standards for your state.		
Assessment contains ratio of multiple choice questions covered on the state assessment.		
Assessment contains questions addressing all the Content Standards for the designated quarter of the Pacing Guide.		
Assessment contains a Pre-Writing Section that the students will use prior to writing to the writing prompt.		
Reading selections are grade appropriate.		
State Test vocabulary is used throughout the assessment.		
Assessment is formatted like the state test.		
Standards are identified for each item.		
Test administration (teacher directions) has been standardized.		
Scoring has been standardized: the writing prompts will be scored using a _____-point holistic applications scale and a _____-point holistic conventions scale. Application scores are double-weighted after scoring; convention scores are not weighted and are added to the total prompt. Multiple choice items are scored as 1 pt. questions.		

Reading Assessment Checklist

School/District _____ Date _____

Grade _____   Assessment # _____

	Yes	No
Assessment contains a fiction piece.		
Assessment contains a nonfiction piece.		
Assessment contains a poem.		
Assessment contains questions addressing all the Content Standards for the designated quarter of the Pacing Guide.		
Assessment contains the appropriate number of multiple choice questions.		
Assessment contains the appropriate number of constructed response questions.		
Assessment contains 5–6 questions per selection. Assessment should have at least 15–25 questions.		
Assessment contains higher-level thinking questions (at least half of the questions).		
Reading selections are grade appropriate.		
State Test vocabulary is used throughout the assessment.		
Assessment is formatted like the State Test.		
Assessment contains charts and graphic organizers.		
Content Standards are identified for each question.		
Test administration (teacher directions) has been standardized.		
Scoring has been standardized (pt. values, specific answers have been given etc.).		

General Assessment Checklist

School/District _____ Date _____

Grade _____ Assessment # _____

	Yes	No
Assessment contains questions addressing all the Content Standards for the designated quarter on the Pacing Guide.		
Assessment contains appropriate number of multiple choice questions.		
Assessment contains appropriate number of constructed response questions.		
Assessment contains 15–25 questions.		
Assessment contains higher-level thinking questions (at least half of the questions).		
Reading level is grade appropriate.		
State Test vocabulary is used throughout the assessment.		
Assessment is formatted like the State Test.		
Assessment contains charts and graphic organizers.		
Content Standards are identified for each question.		
Test administration (teacher directions) has been standardized.		
Scoring has been standardized (pt. values, specific answers have been given, etc.).		

Do Not Disturb

Testing Do Not Disturb

Directions to Read to the Student

Today you will be taking the Short-Cycle Assessment Test. This is a test of how well you understand the material we have covered over the last grading period.

Different types of questions appear on this test: multiple choice, constructed response, and _____ (choose and add any that apply to your state).

All of your answers must be marked or written on your answer sheet.

There are several important things to remember:

1. You may look at any part of the test as often as necessary.

2. Read each question carefully. Think about what is being asked. If a graph or other diagram goes with the question, read it carefully to help you answer the question. Then choose or write the answer that you think is best on your answer sheet.

3. When you are asked to draw or write your answers, draw or write them neatly and clearly in the box provided.

4. When you are asked to select the answer, make sure you fill in the circle next to the answer on your answer sheet. Mark only one answer.

5. If you do not know the answer to a question, skip it and go on. If you have time, remember to return and complete the question.

6. If you finish the test early, you may check over your work. When you are finished and your test booklet and answer sheet have been collected, sit quietly until the time is up. (Other choices may appear here, such as "take out your silent work," etc.)

7. Write or mark your answers directly on your answer sheet. You may not use scratch paper. Use your test sheet to work out problems.

8. You may use the calculator that is provided, if applicable.

Assessment Directions Sheet

Test # _____

Estimated Time: _____

Materials needed:

---

1. Pass out the short-cycle assessment to each student and instruct them to write their names on it. Distribute #2 pencils to students who need them.

2. Say to the students:

You are now going to start your short-cycle assessment for the subject of _____. Please turn to the beginning of your assessment. (Pause.) In this session, you will answer _____ questions. Some of the questions may be hard for you to answer, but it is important that you do your best. If you are not sure of the answer to a question, you should make your best guess. Do not mark your answers in the Question Booklet. Instead, mark your answers for this session in your Student Answer Booklet. Choose the best answer for each multiple-choice question and plan your written answers so they fit only in the answer spaces in your Student Answer Booklet.

Only what you write in the answer spaces in your Student Answer Booklet will be scored. Some questions have more than one part. Try to answer all of the parts. If you are asked to explain or show how you know, be sure to do so. Does anyone have any questions? (Answer any questions the students have about the directions.)

---

3. Say to the students:

It will probably take you about _____ minutes to answer the questions in this session of the test, but you can have more time if you want it. When you are finished with all the questions you may review your answers to the questions.

If you get stuck on a word, I can read the word to you. I cannot read numbers, mathematics symbols, or a whole question to you. If you want help reading a word, raise your hand. (Pronounce the word to students who asked for assistance. Do not define the word or help the students in any other way.) Are there any questions? (Answer any questions the students have about the directions.) When you finish, please sit quietly and read until everyone is finished. You may begin.

The text on pages 157 through 164 provides teachers with graphs to determine percent of mastery on standards. These reports have been imported into an electronic format titled OASIS (Online Student Information Assessment System).

Class Profile Graph

♦ How to use:

- Insert the student names in the provided space at the bottom of the graph.

- Draw a vertical line for the percentage score for each student, coloring it in to create a bar graph.

- Use a black marker and draw a horizontal line at the level that you consider proficient. (Many use a 75% line, however, you can choose to make that higher or lower.)

- Use a purple marker and draw a horizontal line at the percentage that is your class average. To calculate the class average, add all of the percentages together, and divide that number by the number of students who took the assessment. Now, compare the black line and the purple line. This shows the passage rate that you want to achieve and the actual passage rate of your class.

- Use a blue marker and draw a horizontal line at the percentage that is your upper curve line. To calculate this you need to find the standard deviation. To find the standard deviation you take each student's score and subtract it from the mean. For example, if the student scores are

$$64, 32, 56, 89, 91, 55$$

and the mean is 65, then you would subtract:

$$64 - 65 = -1$$
$$32 - 65 = -33$$
$$56 - 65 = -9$$
$$89 - 65 = +24$$
$$91 - 65 = +26$$
$$55 - 65 = -10$$

Next, you square each deficiency:

$$-1 * -1 = 1$$
$$-33 * -33 = 1089$$
$$-9 * -9 = 81$$
$$+24 * +24 = 576$$
$$+26 * +26 = 676$$
$$-10 * -10 = 100$$

Next, take these squares and add them together. It will look like this:

$$1$$
$$1089$$
$$81$$
$$576$$
$$676$$
$$+\ 100\ a$$
$$\overline{2523}$$

Now, divide that sum by the number of scores minus 1. So looking at our work above, that would be 2523 divided by 5 which equals 505.

The last thing you will do is take the square root of this number. That is the standard deviation. In this case the square root of 505 is 22. If you draw a blue line 22 points above your mean of 65 then your upper curve line is 87.

- Use a red marker and draw a horizontal line at the percentage that is your lower curve line. To calculate this use your standard deviation from your upper curve line, which in the case above was 22, and draw your blue line 22 points below the mean of 65 which would place it on 43. Once you have your upper and lower curve lines using a standard deviation of 1, you should understand that, statistically speaking, approximately 68% of your students will fall within the upper and lower curve. Any scores outside of this band, whether above or below, are considered to be statistically different than the rest of the scores. This is where you would look to remediate or enrich. Also, look at the number of students who are clustered right around the 75% line. These are your "bubble" students.

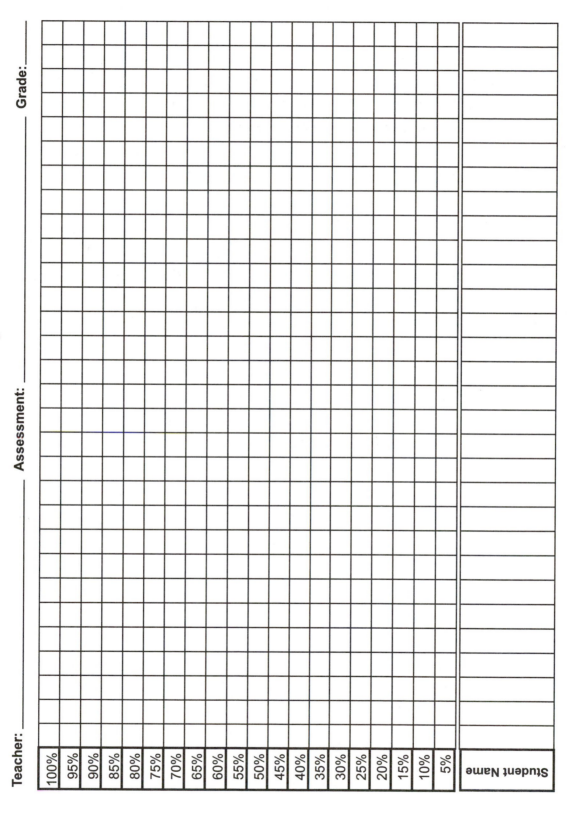

Class Profile Graph

Teacher: _____ Assessment: _____ Grade: _____

Item Analysis Graph

How to use:

♦ Indicate the question number, along with the standard at the bottom of the graph along the y axis, and the percentages 0 to 100 on the x axis.

♦ Score the possible points for a particular question.

- For example, if you have 25 students taking the assessment and the question is worth 1 point, there are 25 possible points.

- Similarly, if there are 25 students and the question is worth 4 points, possible points would be 25 × 4 = 100 points.

♦ Indicate the actual points the class earned.

- For example, if 21 of the 25 students got the 1 point question correct, it is 21 actual points.

♦ To get the % mastered, divide the number of actual points divided by possible points.

- 21 ÷ 25 = .84 or 84%

♦ Color in the bar graph according to the percent mastered.

♦ This will give you an indication of how the class performed overall on each question, as well as classroom successes and gaps.

Classroom Item Analysis Graph

Teacher: _____ Assessment: _____ Grade: _____

Question #	1	2	3	4	5	6	7	8	9	10	11	12	13	14	15	16	17	18	19	20	21	22	23	24	25
Standard																									
100%																									
50%																									
0%																									
Actual Points																									
Possible Points																									
Percent Mastered																									

Non-Mastery Report

How to use:

- ◆ Go through each question and write what standard that question assessed in the blank provided using the coding from the pacing guide.

  - *Example:* Question #1, Standard: M 2–5

- ◆ In the lines provided, you may write out the standard for a reference to what the standard was covering. You may want to write the descriptor out word for word, or you may want to write a 1 to 2 word descriptor of it.

  - *Example:* Analyze problem situations involving measurement concepts, select appropriate strategies, and use an organized approach to solve narrative and increasingly complex problems.

- ◆ In the box provided, write all the names of the students in your class who did not master that particular question.

  - Remember that mastery for a constructed response questions means the student gets a 75% or above.

    Example:

      3 points out of 4 is mastery

      2 points out of 4 is non-mastery

    Example:

      2 points out of 2 is mastery

      1 point out of 2 is non-mastery

- ◆ Go through all the questions placing the names of the students who did not master the question in the appropriate box.

- ◆ This list will give you an indication of how you can group students in your class if you need to go back and reteach a standard. This will also inform you which standard(s) you will need to reteach to the entire class, or if you need to go further into depth on a certain standard.

Non-Mastery Report

Question #_____, Standard _____

_____

_____

_____

Question #_____, Standard _____

_____

_____

_____

Question #_____, Standard _____

_____

_____

_____

Individual Assessment Reflection

The students were most successful with which standard? (Classroom Item Analysis Graph)	
The students had the most difficulty with which standard? (Classroom Item Analysis Graph)	
Describe the questions the students had the most success with: multiple choice, constructed response, lower level, higher level, etc. (Short-cycle assessment)	
Describe the questions the students had the most difficulty with: multiple choice, constructed response, lower level, higher level, etc. (Short-cycle assessment)	
Looking at individual students, were there capable students who did not do well? Please list them. Implications? (Class Profile Graph)	
Looking at individual students, were there less-capable students who did better than you thought they would? Please list them. Implications? (Class Profile Graph)	
Were you satisfied overall with your classroom performance on this assessment? Explain. (Class Profile Graph)	
Were you satisfied overall with your grade-level performance on this assessment? Explain. (All Class Profile Graphs)	
Compare your class bar graph with the other classes level bar graph (if applicable). Comments? (All Class Profile Graphs)	
After reviewing the results, are there areas/types of questions/standards that you think need to be differentiated? What are they?	
What specific implications do you see for instruction during the next grading period? What will you do differently to change the results of the next assessment?	

Group Data Analysis for Assessment #1

Based upon data gathered regarding student performance on short-cycle assess-ments.

5 Most *Successful Test Items from Assessment*				5 Least *Successful Test Items from Assessment*			
Item #	Standard	Specific Level of Bloom's Taxonomy	Kind of Question	Item #	Standard	Specific Level of Bloom's Taxonomy	Kind of Question

Instructional Implications: (Please list. Be as specific as possible.)

Once you have filled the analysis out, check to be sure none of the least successful questions were a result of a question that was not clear or was not written to your satisfaction. If that is the case, revise the test.

Group Data Analysis for Assessment #2

Based upon data gathered regarding student performance on short-cycle assessments.

5 Most *Successful Test Items from Assessment*				5 Least *Successful Test Items from Assessment*			
Item #	Standard	Specific Level of Bloom's Taxonomy	Kind of Question	Item #	Standard	Specific Level of Bloom's Taxonomy	Kind of Question

How much time (approximate) was spent on instructing each successful item? On each of the least successful items? What is the relationship between the instruction time and the performance on the indicator?

What are the performance trends regarding the thinking skill level of the questions? How did the thinking skill level impact student performance?

Goals: Establish three instructional goals based upon the data you have analyzed for the next 9 weeks.

Strategies: For each goal, how will you implement strategies to achieve them?

Group Data Analysis for Assessment #3

Based upon data gathered regarding student performance on short-cycle assessments.

5 Most *Successful Test Items from Assessment*				5 Least *Successful Test Items from Assessment*			
Item #	Standard	Specific Level of Bloom's Taxonomy	Kind of Question	Item #	Standard	Specific Level of Bloom's Taxonomy	Kind of Question

What about your changes in instruction have caused students to improve their scores this year?

What are some future instructional implications? (Be as specific as possible.)

What are three goals you could set for the final assessment?

1.

2.

3.

Group Data Analysis for Assessment #4

Based upon data gathered regarding student performance on short-cycle assessments.

5 Most *Successful Test Items from Assessment*				5 Least *Successful Test Items from Assessment*			
Item #	Standard	Specific Level of Bloom's Taxonomy	Kind of Question	Item #	Standard	Specific Level of Bloom's Taxonomy	Kind of Question

Look at the results of Assessment # 4 for your grade level. Does any of the data confirm the qualitative data represented in the "Wish List/Bet Your Paycheck" vertical alignment activity? Please explain.

Are there specific standards that you feel the students have completely mastered based on the data? What are they?

Are there specific standards that you feel the students have not mastered based on the data? What are they?

What is one thing you would let next year's teacher know with regard to instruction based on your data? Please explain in detail.

How Did You Learn What Was Taught?

Think of something that you have learned that has become a lifelong activity or skill. How was it taught to you? How did you learn it? Were they one and the same?

Fill out the chart below describing the process of teaching and learning as it relates to your activity or skill.

Activity or Skill: _____

How It Was Taught	*How It Was Learned*

SMART Goals

SMART Goal	Indicators	Measurement	Targets
Specific and strategic, measurable, attainable, results-oriented, time bound.	Standards and objectives for gaps in performance (what is not there, not measured, or not acceptable…).	Tools you will use to determine improvement from where your school is now to whether they are improving.	The attainable performance level that you would like to see by a given time.
Smart Goal	Indicators	Measurement Method	Target for Measurement
		Measurement Method	Target for Measurement

Differentiated Instruction

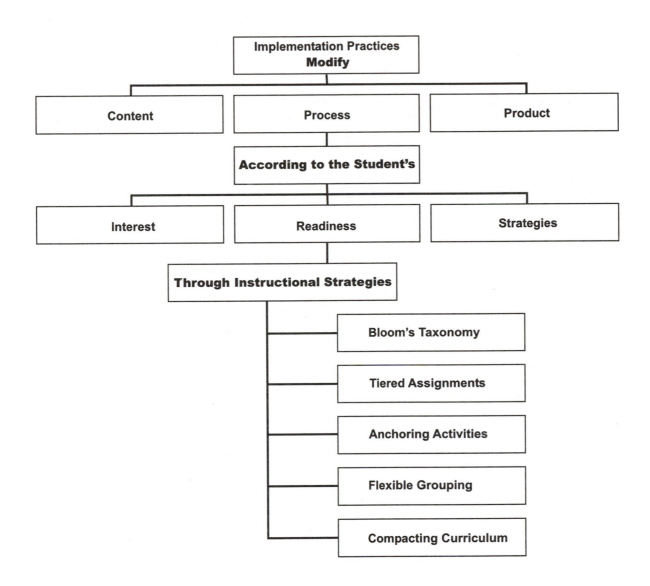

Compensation Strategies
for Special Education Students

The following is a list of compensation strategies that can be easily used with special education students to help them when attempting grade-level work.

- Teach students to always read the captions, subtitles, and headings of a selection before attempting to read the text. This will help direct their understanding.

- If there are questions with the selection, teach students to read the questions prior to reading the selection. This will help their comprehension and direct their reading. Likewise, if the questions are to be read to the student, read them before the student attempts to read the text.

- Have the students highlight all of the words that they can already read prior to attempting to read grade-appropriate text. The student will find that in most cases, more than half of the text will be highlighted. This will increase confidence before they even attempt to read the selection.

- Teach the students to restate the question in their answer. Many times we do not do this, as writing is usually difficult for the special education student. However, many times these students are not successful answering questions because they don't actually know what the question is asking. Restating the question in their answer will strengthen comprehension of the text.

- Tape record the selection ahead of time and have the student listen to it as they read it silently.

- Purchase the "hearing horns" that are commercially available which allows the student to read aloud by whispering the text and hearing it back through the hearing aid.

- Chunk the material for the student. Only provide part of the text to them at a time; this will lessen the confusion for them and help to avoid overwhelming them.

- Have the students circle all of the important words in the selection as they read. These words may be related to the main idea, or they may be directional words such as "two examples" or "explain why," etc.

- Provide the students with graphic organizers whenever possible. For example, a story web with a circle for the main idea, and smaller circles for the supporting details that the students can fill out as they read, will strengthen comprehension.

- Provide word banks for the students that have been prepared ahead of time. This will help them when they come to important words that they do not know. Also, this will allow them to get the help they need independently, and therefore not break up the flow of their reading.

- In Math, teach the students how to use a calculator, and allow them to use it as often as they need to. Some of these students may never learn the basic facts, and teaching them to use a calculator may truly be one of the most important skills they learn in Math.

Rubric

Excellent			
Good			
Needs Improvement			

Project Contract

Student Name: _____

Project Name: _____

Estimated Time of Project: _____
    (Include calendar)

Standards Covered:

_____

_____

_____

_____

Skills Learned:

    ◆

    ◆

    ◆

    ◆

Overall Goal of Project: _____

_____

_____

Product of Project: _____

_____

Headings for Rubric Evaluation: _____

_____

    (include rubric)

Student Signature: _____

Teacher Signature: _____

Parent(s) Signature: _____

References

Alaska Department of Education and Early Childhood. Alaska 6-Point Rubric.

Bennett, R. E., & Ward, W. C. (1993). *Construction versus choice in cognitive measurement: Issues in constructed response, performance testing, and portfolio assessment.* Mahwah, NJ: Lawrence Erlbaum Associates.

Briscoe, C. (1996). The teacher as learner: Interpretations from a case study of teacher change. *Journal of Curriculum Studies,* 28, 315–329.

Brookover, W. B., & Lezotte, L. W. (1979). *Changes in school characteristics coincident with changes in student achievement.* East Lansing, MI: Michigan State University, College of Urban Development, (ED181005).

Cochran-Smith, M., & S.L. Lytle. (1993). *Inside/outside: Teacher research and knowledge.* New York: Teachers College Press.

Costigan, A. T., Crocco, M. S., Zumwalt, K. K. (2004). *Learning to teach in an age of accountability.* Mahwah, NJ: Lawrence Erlbaum Associates.

Darling-Hammond, L. (1994). *Professional Developments Schools: Schools for Developing a Profession.* New York: Teachers College Press.

Darling-Hammond, L. (1999). *Teacher quality and student achievement: A review of state policy evidence.* Seattle, WA: Center for the Study of Teaching and Policy, University of Washington.

Davidson, N. (1994). Cooperative and collaborative learning: An integrated perspective. In J. Thousand, R. Villa, & A. Nevin (Eds.), *Creativity and collaborative learning: A practical guide to empowering students and teachers* (pp. 13–30). Baltimore: Paul H. Brooks.

Edmonds, R. R. (1979). Some schools work and more can. *Social Policy 9,* 28–32.

Firestone, W. A., Schorr, R. Y., & Monfils, L. F. (Eds.). (2004). *The ambiguity of teaching to the test: Standards, assessment, and educational reform.* Mahwah, NJ: Lawrence Erlbaum.

Florida Department of Education. Florida Comprehensive Assessment Test (FCAT).

Gallagher, P. Managing Educational Change: The Concerns-Based Adoption Model (CBAM) in Reform, Learner.org, http://64.233.161.104/search?q=cache: mLdFZKf55qsJ:www.learner.org/theguide/Cbam.html+%22Innovation+Configurations,+Stages+of+Concern,+and+Levels+of+Use%22&hl=en&ie=UTF-8

Killion, J. (2002). *Assessing impact: Evaluating staff development.* Oxford, OH: National Staff Development Council.

Klopp, P. (1976). *The Wisconsin design for reading skill development; A report on the 1973–74 small scale field test.* Madison, WI: Wisconsin Research and Development Center for Cognitive Learning and Instruction, University of Wisconsin.

Locke, E.A. & Latham, G.P. (1990). *A theory of goal seeking and task performance.* Englewood Cliff, NJ: Prentice Hall.

Loucks-Horsley, S. (1996). The concerns-based adoption model (CBAM): A model for change in individuals. In R. Bybee (Ed.), *National standards & the science curriculum.* Dubuque, Iowa: Kendall/Hunt Publishing Co.

Madaus G. F., & Stufflebeam D. (Eds.). (1989). *Educational evaluation: Classic works of Ralph Tyler.* Boston: Kluwer.

Shepard, L. A. (2002, April). Why we need better assessments. *Educational Leadership, 46(7),* 4–9.

Simmons, W., & Resnich, L. (1993). Assessment as the catalyst of school reform. *Educational Leadership, 50(5),* 11–15.

Stufflebeam, D.L. (1969). Evaluation as enlightenment for decision-making. In W.A. Beaty (Ed.), *Improving assessment and an inventory of measures of affective behavior.* Washington, DC: Association for Supervision and Curriculum Development.

Stufflebeam, D. (2001). *Evaluation models: New directions for evaluation.* Jossey-Bass.

Vermont Department of Education. New England Common Assessment Program (NECAP).

Wholey, J. S. (1979) *Evaluation: Promise and performance.* Washington, DC: The Urban Institute: Author.

Wholey, J. S. (1983). *Evaluation and effective public management.* Boston: Little, Brown, & Co.

Wholey, J. S. (1987). Evaluability assessment: Developing program theory. In L. Bickman (Ed.), *Using program theory in evaluation. New Directions for Program Evaluation,* No. 33. San Francisco: Jossey-Bass.

Wiggins, G., & Irua, L. (1997). *Educative assessment: Designing assessments to inform and improve student performance,* Jossey-Bass Inc.

Wiggins,G., & McTighe, J. (1998). *Understanding by design.* Alexandria, VA: Association of Supervision and Curriculum Development.

Wiggins,G. (1998). A true test. Toward more authentic and equitable assessment. *Phi Delta Kappan, 70.*

Wholey, J. S. (1987). Evaluability assessment: Developing program theory. In L. Bickman (Ed.), *Using program theory in evaluation.* New Directions for Program Evaluation, No. 33. San Francisco: Jossey-Bass.